Sheed

What the experts are saying about *Wine Savvy:*

"An encounter with a wine list is for many people a white-knuckle experience on the order of an IRS audit. *Wine Savvy* does a splendid job of instilling courage and confidence in the eno-timid."

Randall Grahm, winemaker,
Bonny Doon Vineyard

"With wit and simplicity, the author leads readers through the maze of supposed wine mysteries."

The Oregonian

"In her unintimidating, conversational style, Heidi Yorkshire has cracked the code of understanding wine."

Antonia Allegra, author,
Napa Valley: The Ultimate Winery Guide

"A book that packs more useful information for beginners into 105 pages than any other."

Adventures in Dining

"Remarkably lucid and down-to-earth. *Wine Savvy* will boost many a wine beginner to higher levels of enjoyment and connoisseurship."

David Rosengarten, co-author,
Red Wine with Fish: The New Art of Matching Wine with Food

"A commonsense guide to wine appreciation that captures the essence of wine's inherent charm."

Napa Valley Appellation

"The new national primer for basic wine education. Witty, warm and well-researched. Everyone interested in wine should read this book."

Jeff Prather, co-author, *Northwest Wines*

WINE SAVVY

The Simple Guide
to Buying and Enjoying Wine
Anytime, Anywhere

by Heidi Yorkshire

With a Foreword by Robert Mondavi

Duplex Media Group
Portland, Oregon

WINE SAVVY

The Simple Guide to Buying and Enjoying Wine Anytime, Anywhere

Revised Edition

published by

Duplex Media Group
Post Office Box 12081
Portland OR 97212-0081 U.S.A.

Publishers Cataloging-in-Publication Data

Yorkshire, Heidi, 1952-
  Wine savvy : the simple guide to buying and
enjoying wine anytime, anywhere / Heidi
Yorkshire. — Portland, Or. : Duplex Media
Group, c1994 and 1996.

        p. : ill. ; cm.

        Includes bibliographical references and
  index.

        1. Wine and wine making.   I. Title.
TP548.Y   641.22 dc20

ISBN 1-883970-16-4: $12.95 Softcover

Book and cover design by Tom Hardy.

Cover photograph by John Rizzo.

In memory of

Andrea Boroff Eagan

Foreword

I always knew we had the soils, the grape varieties and the climates here in America that would allow us to make wines that rank with the best in the world. And I was fortunate to start in Napa Valley, with its consistent climate and a nucleus of energetic and committed people. Now good wines are made in many parts of this country and many areas of the world — I have been to most of them and tasted the results. We're all making progress, and in the next few years we're going to accomplish amazing things!

But winemakers aren't satisfied to simply make wonderful wines and have them sit in the bottles. We're only truly fulfilled when appreciative people open the bottles and savor a glass or two. *Wine Savvy* is a delightful book that will help more people learn to appreciate and enjoy the wines that we make. One of the best aspects of the book is that the information in it applies to buying and drinking wines from all over the world — they have so much in common.

Heidi Yorkshire has done a fine job of telling the complicated story of wine in an easy-to-read and interesting way. We winemakers sometimes make wine sound so complicated, when the reality is that a bottle of wine is a simple, lovely and perfectly natural accompaniment to a meal.

Read, and you'll enjoy the presentation. Then share a glass, and you'll enjoy the experience. I promise!

ROBERT MONDAVI
NAPA VALLEY

Acknowledgements

Among the many friends and colleagues who were remarkably generous with time, expertise and encouragement throughout the writing and publishing of this book are: Jo Robinson, Leslie Cole, Randall Grahm, Bernard Ohanian, Sandra Dorr, Matthew Elsen, Bob Liner, Susan Sokol Blosser and Joseph and Janice Nase.

Without the creativity and patience of graphic designer Tom Hardy, this book would still be on disk.

The chart of New World-Old World equivalents in Chapter 6 is courtesy of Joseph Nase. The table pairing wine varieties with herbs and spices in Chapter 10 is based on *Food and Wine of the Pacific Northwest* by John Sarich, culinary director of Chateau Ste. Michelle, and on an interview with chef Greg Higgins. Stephen Lawrence of Clicquot, Inc. provided information on his great love, Champagne. Jeff Prather of Ray's Boathouse contributed his eagle eye and foolproof method of using a corkscrew. Evan Goldstein of Sterling Vineyards School of Service and Hospitality added his insights on food and wine combinations. Professor Linda Bartoshuk of the Yale University Medical School explained the physiology of taste. Chuck Hill of the Pacific Northwest Enological Society added thoughts on wine-tasting groups.

Shinzen Young and Robert Beatty were simply essential.

Special appreciation goes to John Rizzo for his wonderful photography and good humor.

Affectionate thanks are due to my almost-uncle John Morrissey and my uncle Herbert Berk, for their interest and help.

My parents, Analee and Boris Yorkshire, have supported me lovingly and unconditionally for as long as I can remember. And my husband, Joseph Anthony, is a true partner in every sense of the word.

HEIDI YORKSHIRE
PORTLAND, OREGON

Contents

Good Taste Is Your Taste

A glass of wine can bring a lot of pleasure to life. Maybe you've experienced the magic during a quiet dinner at the beginning of a romance, at a summer barbecue with old friends, or sitting in the sun on a cafe terrace in Aix-en-Provence or San Francisco. The wine didn't make it happen, exactly, but it added something — a feeling of well-being, a moment of connection, an awakening of the senses — that you'd like to enjoy again.

Unfortunately, such moments seem awfully distant when you're standing in a wine shop full of unfamiliar labels, browsing through a supermarket wine department with no help in sight, or peering at a restaurant wine list that's about as thick as the Manhattan phone book.

Wouldn't it be great if you could feel as comfortable buying wine as you do buying, say, ice cream? After all, one carton of Rocky Road tastes pretty much like every other carton of Rocky Road. You never have to worry about whether Strawberries 'n' Cream will impress your guests more than Chocolate Fudge Ripple. You never see two almost-identical cartons of ice cream next to each other on the shelf with price tags reading $4.99 and $49.99. If you're like most people, you know what ice cream tastes like, you know your favorite flavor, you know how much you're willing to spend and, as they say in the athletic shoe commercials, you just do it. Damn the butterfat, full speed ahead!

Of course, wine is not ice cream. It'll never be so simple. But it doesn't have to be so confusing, either.

This book is designed to help you gain confidence in your own taste, without anyone else's opinions or prejudices getting in the way, including mine. You'll learn how to recognize the aromas and sensations that make you love a wine. You'll get over any idea that you have to be rich to experience truly fine wines (although a little money never hurts). And you'll soon have enough basic, common-sense knowledge to make buying and drinking wine as full of pleasant anticipation and gratifying rewards as buying and eating ice cream.

Most of all, you can use this book to define your own taste and learn to express it. By trusting yourself and having confidence in your experience, you get much more than something to drink. You'll have the pleasure of realizing that good taste and your taste are one and the same.

It's impossible to avoid generalizing, but I've tried to make the general rules as useful as possible. Among the thousands of variables possible in the wine world, there'll certainly be an exception — somewhere, somehow — to just about everything. Wine nuts love to rattle on about an obscure little grape from Portugal or a new wrinkle in fermentation on the Austro-Hungarian border. I've kept the focus firmly on wines you're likely to encounter in wine shops and on restaurant wine lists in North America.

Tuning In to Your Senses

Very few people actually pay attention, careful attention, to what they eat or drink. They look at a dish, give it a name — "That's a cheeseburger" — and then they eat it, expecting the dish to taste like the thing they named. That's not tasting; that's flying on a kind of culinary automatic pilot, which is what most of us do, most of the time. But once in a great while, some aspect of that cheeseburger will taste so delicious or weird that it will truly attract our attention: maybe it's got blue cheese instead of cheddar, too much salt, or a slice of grilled pineapple on top.

Drinking wine is like eating a cheeseburger. You're using the same physical equipment, and you're deciding thumbs up or thumbs down. But unless you've paid a lot of attention when you've been drinking wine in the past, you probably don't have a very clear notion of what a wine should taste like, or what makes it good or bad. The flavors in wine are far more subtle than in most foods. Therefore, it takes some practice to distinguish between wines, to decide what you like, or even to remember what's what.

If you've ever had your house painted and tried to pick out a color for the living room, you already know something about subtle distinctions. Who ever thought there were so many shades of white until you saw them all lined up in one place? Those very small differences are the visual equivalent of the taste differences among many wines.

Wine professionals — the so-called wine experts — learn to recognize such differences because they taste tens of thousands of wines during their careers. But you don't have to taste a thousand wines a year to learn to do the same thing. You have the basic qualifications already: a sense of taste and a sense of smell. There's nothing mysterious about it. Nobody, not even the seventh son of the seventh son of a French winemaker, springs from the womb with the mystical ability to tell Chateau Latour from Chateau Lafite, or even Chateau Latour from Thunderbird.

What's All That Sniffing and Slurping About?

All your taste is *not* in your mouth. It's also in your nose and, especially, your brain. Of course, your taste buds, many thousands of them, are on your tongue. But they're only receptors of stimuli, just like your eyes or your skin. Several nerves connect the taste buds to the brain, which is where you make the actual decisions and judgments about how something tastes — and whether you like it.

You may have read in a physiology text or another wine book that the tongue is divided into zones where the taste buds taste only sweet, sour, bitter or salty flavors. That's wrong. In fact, all the taste buds taste all four flavors.

Using your mouth alone, you can only distinguish among four different tastes: sweet, salty, sour (acidic) and bitter. But many tastes are complicated, multi-layered. How do you sense the nuances of a ripe apricot, a rare grilled steak, a green chile enchilada with tomatillo salsa, or a glass of Merlot? The answer is as plain as the nose on your face.

The *olfactory* sense — the sense of smell — is miraculously complex; it's far more sensitive to odors than our tongue is to flavors. Humans can recognize many more scents than tastes. When it comes to wine, that's good, because much of what makes wine interesting and delicious is embodied in how it smells — what is called its *nose* or *bouquet*. That's where many of the subtle distinctions between wines become apparent.

Now . . . Take a Deep Breath

Wine smells like grapes, of course. It also smells like many other things. For example, some red wines evoke blackberries, mushrooms or tobacco; some white wines give hints of fresh-cut grass, ripe melon or crisp green apple. But winemakers don't dump berries or apples into the tank along with the grapes, even though it may sound that way.

Wine is made from grapes. The wonderful scents that waft past your nose come from *esters,* compounds of acid and alcohol that form in wine and carry its aromatic qualities. (Wine can also be made from many other foods that can be fermented, such as rice — that's Japanese *sake* — blackberries and dandelions. But the only wine I'm talking about in this book is made from grapes.)

Exactly what you smell depends on the many variables involved in winemaking, among them the type of grape used, where it was grown or if it was aged in oak barrels. It also matters how long it's been in the bottle (esters can continue to form over many years), and even what other plants were growing near the vineyard, like lavender in the south of France or eucalyptus in parts of California.

At first, you may not find many scintillating scents in wine. The aromas are subtle, and to detect them, you need to be very familiar with their stronger, everyday form. If you haven't tried it lately, take the time to crush a sprig of fresh thyme in your hand and inhale the aroma, or slowly savor a dish of sun-warmed raspberries. Bury your nose in a bouquet of violets, or take a deep whiff of vanilla or cedar, a just-cut lemon or a crumpled eucalyptus leaf.

Sensitivity to the nuances of smell comes with practice. If you want to get in training for wine appreciation, go to the supermarket, wander around the produce section, pick up the melons, berries, ripe pears and bundles of herbs, and inhale deeply. You may get thrown out for odd behavior. But you'll sharpen up your senses for the scents that appear in wine. Those sharpened senses will probably help you enjoy eating more, too.

Another way to practice recognizing aromas in wine is to take small glasses of a white wine without much

> *Try this simple experiment to prove how important your nose is to your sense of taste. Close your eyes and hold your nose. Let a friend give you a piece of apple and a piece of pear. Taste them. Can you tell the fruits apart without being able to smell them? Most people can't. It's through the nose that we get the most information about the foods we eat.*

> *"If you want to know about a tree, go to the tree."*
>
> Basho,
> 17th century
> haiku master

5

bouquet and add various scents to them. Try a few drops of vanilla extract, a piece of pear, a couple of raspberries, even some fresh-mown grass. You'll smell the aromas in a way that's very similar to how they naturally occur in wine.

"I do fine in the arena of household smells. I can tell when to change the litter in the cat box. I know when the toast is burnt even before I pop it up. I know when the emergency brake on the car didn't release. [But during wine tastings], I'm always thinking of things like Mentholatum, macaroons, and oatmeal . . . while other people mention delicate and worldly scents like licorice, lightly toasted French oak and new-mown alfalfa. I stick my nose in my glass and try to imagine that I smell whatever it is, too. Sometimes this works, especially if you tell me a wine smells like Luden's cough drops."

Jenni Green, St. Innocent Winery, Oregon

3

How Wine Tastes

"I like my barbecued ribs spicy, not sweet."
"That chocolate cake is too sugary and not chocolatey enough."
"Sharp cheddar cheese makes better macaroni and cheese than bland American cheese."

Whenever you make such a judgment, you're expressing preferences developed over a whole lifetime of eating. But when it comes to expressing preferences about wine, a problem often arises: not being able to describe what you like well enough to find it.

That's why this chapter will focus on some of the important elements that determine, to a great extent, what wine tastes like. Once you can recognize these elements, you'll have a basic personal framework for knowing what wines you prefer, and a vocabulary in common with wine merchants, waiters and fellow wine lovers, so you can understand each other.

There's More to Wine Than "Dry"

After *white* and *red,* most people's wine vocabulary stops with *dry.* Certainly, a dry wine (a wine that does not taste obviously sweet) is appropriate with most foods. For myself, I don't want a sugary wine with my roast beef any more than I'd want a cola or a strawberry milkshake. Yet simply asking for a dry wine doesn't help much to narrow down the huge field of wines. Wines that are made to go with food — and that means virtually all good table wines — *are* dry, or have only a tiny bit of sweetness to them.

In fact, when people ask for a dry wine, what they're probably talking about is their preference about how a wine balances several essential elements:

- **tannin**
- **sweetness/fruitiness**
- **acidity/crispness**
- **alcohol**

The exercise below will teach you how to pinpoint these characteristics in wine. It will also take a slight detour to give a simple illustration of how important texture, the feeling of the wine in the mouth, can be.

World's Cheapest Tasting Exercise: The Tea Tasting

It's amazing! It's incredible! It's possible to focus on the flavors and sensations of drinking wine — without spending any money on wine! (Good thing, too. Who can afford to open up bottles of wine just for a tasting exercise?) With ordinary black tea and a couple of other common kitchen ingredients, you can learn to recognize some of the most basic qualities of wine.

Ingredients

- 2-3 teabags of black tea (Lipton or similar)
- 4 teaspoons granulated sugar
- lemon juice or a whole lemon
- a tablespoon or two of heavy cream
- a few plain crackers or cubes of French bread

This ingenious exercise is the brainchild of Tim Hanni of Beringer Vineyards in the Napa Valley. Hanni, a Master of Wine, originally devised it to teach teetotaling waiters to recommend wines to their customers.

Preparations

1. Fill a 2-cup (16-ounce) measuring cup with boiling water and use all the teabags to brew some very strong tea. Let it cool to room temperature.

2. Pour roughly equal amounts of tea into four glasses. Set the four glasses in a row, and think of them, from left to right, as #1, #2, #3, and #4. Number them if you like.

3. Add 2 teaspoons sugar to glass #2, and stir to dissolve.

4. Add 2 teaspoons sugar to glass #3, and stir to dissolve.

Glass #1 — Tannin

1. Take a mouthful from #1. Swish the tea around in your mouth before swallowing.

2. Now run your tongue over your teeth and along the roof of your mouth. What do you feel? If the tea was good and strong, you will probably feel a puckery, gritty, almost sandpapery sensation in your mouth, especially on your teeth. Your mouth could also feel dry, as if the moisture has been sucked out. You may also taste a bitterness on the back of your tongue.

3. Pretend you're at a snooty wine tasting, and nibble on a cracker or piece of bread to clear your palate.

You've just experienced the distinctive taste and feeling of *tannin*. Tannin is present in strong tea, and it's also present in the skins, seeds and stems of wine grapes. When you bite into a grape with seeds, that gritty feeling between your teeth is tannin. In general, the longer the skins and seeds (and sometimes stems) of grapes remain in contact with grape juice that's being made into wine, the more tannin the wine will contain.

Wine grapes come in many colors, from green to pink to red to purple so deep that it's almost black, but when you squeeze most grapes the juice runs clear. Wine gets its color from grape skins. Red wines almost always

> *"To know a thing, you must know the opposite . . . just as much, else you don't know that one thing."*
>
> Henry Moore, sculptor

contain more tannin than white wines because they spend more time in contact with the grape skins.

A little tannin is essential in all wine. It contributes to what is called the wine's structure and enhances its aromatic qualities. The dryness or roughness you felt in your mouth when you drank the strong tea is tannin's astringency. Red wines, with their stronger flavors, can support some astringency. In white wines, however, winemakers have to carefully limit the amount of tannin to keep the wine's delicate flavors from being overwhelmed by astringent tannins.

The presence of tannin is also a factor that can allow a wine to age successfully. Red wines that are meant to be aged sometimes taste somewhat rough and tannic when young.

4. Take another sip of #1 to fix the taste and sensation of tannin in your memory.

5. Clear your palate with a bite of bread or a mouthful of water.

Glass #2 — Sweetness

1. Take a mouthful from #2. Swish the tea around in your mouth before swallowing.

2. What do you taste first, the sweetness or the tannin? This glass of tea is as strong as #1, but does it taste as strong or as tannic? Take another mouthful and pay attention to how the two elements — the sweetness and the tannin — interact. Does one overpower the other?

3. After you swallow, take note of the flavors that remain in your mouth. Is there any sort of aftertaste? How about other sensations?

4. Taste #2 again, to fix the taste and sensation of sweetness in your memory.

5. Eat a piece of bread or drink some water to clear your palate.

Sweetness, or the impression of sweetness, is another key element in creating the taste of wine. It all goes back to the fact that wine is made from grapes, and grapes are fruit. Like most fruits, they become sweeter as they ripen in the sun.

Fermentation can't happen without sugar. Yeast needs to feed on something so it can grow. If you stir yeast into plain water, it just sits there, but if you add a spoonful of sugar, the yeast comes alive, and things start to bubble. During fermentation, yeast turns sugar to alcohol.

The amount of sugar in grapes depends on a number of factors. Grapes that grow in very hot, southern climates tend to be sweeter than those grown in cooler, northern climates. For some types of wine, winemakers prefer the grapes to be very high in sugar, while for others, lower levels of sugar are better. But starting with very ripe, sweet grapes does not necessarily mean that a wine will be sweet. Instead, it only means that the wine is potentially higher in alcohol.

In a dry wine, no sugar, or almost none, remains after fermentation — the yeasts have turned it all to alcohol. Most fine table wines are fermented until they're completely dry, or have a tiny, almost imperceptible, bit of sugar remaining in them, barely enough to bring out the flavor of the grapes. A wine that contains just a little more sugar — enough that you can taste it — is called *off-dry.* A winemaker can control the amount of sugar that remains in wine by raising or lowering the temperature as it ferments to kill the yeasts and stop fermentation.

Even though dry wines contain little or no sugar, the fact remains that some of them give an impression of sweetness, especially in the nose. Much of that impression is caused by hints of various fruit aromas in wine, such as grape, apple, pear, berry, cherry or even pineapple, to name just a few. (What aromas you might smell is determined by many variables, especially the variety of grape from which the wine is made, the fermentation temperature, and the type of yeast used.) Overall, that impression is called *fruitiness.* Sensory researchers say that human beings interpret fruity aromas as "sweet" because they have learned to associate the aroma of fruit automatically with the taste of sweetness.

Other aromas in dry wine are not considered part of its fruitiness, but can also fool you into thinking the wine's sweet. If a wine is aged in oak barrels, it can pick up the scents of vanilla or clove, which most of us connect with sweet desserts. Some wines even have a buttery or butterscotch smell, caused by a certain fermentation process.

If you're not sure whether a wine contains sugar, check the label on the bottle; it may tell you if the wine contains *residual sugar,* which is any significant amount left over after fermentation. The amount of sugar is often expressed as a percentage; for example, ".6 percent residual sugar." Scientists say that we begin to perceive the taste of sugar in wine when it reaches about .4 percent. Above about 2 percent, the wine will have a noticeably sweet but not syrupy taste. Dessert wines, which are very sweet, can contain as much as 15 percent residual sugar, or sometimes more.

So, the next time a table wine seems sweet to you, spend a few moments trying to analyze its aromas. Then taste carefully. You may want to hold your nose so that you're not strongly swayed by the smells. You'll probably be able to confirm that the wine contains no sugar, or practically none. The "sweetness" that you're experiencing is the fruitiness of the nose instead, or other aromas that develop during the winemaking process.

Glass #3 — Acidity

1.Squeeze a couple of teaspoons of lemon juice into #3. Stir to mix. Now, take a sip.

2. Does #3 taste as sweet as #2, which contained the same amount of sugar? How has the addition of lemon changed the way you perceive the sweetness? How do the sweetness of the sugar and the acidity of the lemon interact?

Acidity is the third key element in the taste of wine. Acidity gives wines their zingy, fresh quality, and balances out sweetness or fruitiness with a refreshing crispness. Chances are, sample #3 didn't taste as sweet to you as #2, even though they both contain the same amount of sugar. The acid in the lemon juice has cut through the sweetness.

Often, when people complain that a wine is "too sweet," what they're really sensing is that it isn't crisp enough, that it doesn't have enough acidity to balance its fruity qualities. But too much acidity can make a wine taste sour and thin. Finding an equilibrium between sweetness and acidity is one of the winemaker's balancing acts.

3. Which glass do you prefer, #2 or #3?

4. Eat a piece of bread or drink some water to clear your palate.

Glass #4—Texture

1. Stir a good dollop of cream into #4. Take a sip and swirl it around in your mouth.

2. How does the cream change the taste of the tea? How does it change the way the tea feels in your mouth?

The texture of a wine in your mouth is another key to whether you enjoy it. A liquid can create diverse physical sensations, smooth and creamy, say, rather than sharp or rough. Some wines feel big and velvety, some are enjoyably prickly (sparkling wine perhaps the best example), and some are thin and refreshing.

Of course, nobody puts dairy products in wine (although skim milk is sometimes used to clarify wine during the winemaking process). But some wines undergo a second fermentation, called *malolactic fermentation,* which changes *malic acid,* a sharp-tasting acid found in grapes (and apples and rhubarb), to *lactic acid,* a mellower-tasting acid which is found in dairy products. Malolactic fermentation can be a factor in making a wine feel creamier in your mouth.

3. Taste #3 and then #4. Compare the feeling in your mouth of the lemon juice in #3 and the cream in #4.

4. Go back and taste #1, and compare it with #4. How do they differ?

5. Eat a piece of bread or swish some water around in your mouth.

Alcohol: More than a Feeling

If you've ever tasted a high-alcohol spirit like whiskey or vodka, it probably felt "hot" or searing, and made your mouth burn a bit. It also probably seemed a bit thicker or denser in your mouth than water would, because alcohol has a slightly thick texture, especially when very cold, as anyone who's ever put a bottle of vodka in the freezer can tell you.

Although wine contains far less alcohol than spirits, alcohol in wine creates similar effects, sometimes adding hotness to the wine, sometimes a sense of thickness or body. Different wines contain different percentages of alcohol. Again, the variations are caused by a number of factors, but primarily by the ripeness of the grapes used. (Riper grapes are higher in sugar, which usually results in wines higher in alcohol.) Sunny wine-growing regions like southern France, Italy, Spain and parts of California produce very ripe grapes, and the wines are often high in alcohol, as much as 13 or 14 percent. In contrast, wines from Germany, where the weather is cooler, can be as low as 7.5 percent alcohol. You will usually find the percentage of alcohol on the label of a wine bottle. Although these differences seem small, they are definitely perceptible as you become sensitive to them.

Pure Tastes

Experiencing these four tastes — *tannin, sweetness, acidity* and *alcohol* — in a pure form gives you a good base for understanding why you do or don't like a certain wine.

For example, if you try a wine that feels rough or astringent in your mouth and leaves a bitter aftertaste, you'll realize that it has more tannin than you like. If it seems "hot," it may contain too much alcohol for your taste. If a wine makes you pucker up, maybe it's too acidic for you; on the other hand, if it tastes rather flat but not sweet, perhaps it isn't acidic enough. You'll know how to differentiate between a wine that's actually sweet and one that's just fruity.

Keeping these four elements in mind, you'll be able to communicate more precisely what you want in a wine, and you'll have a far greater chance of getting it.

Favorite Food and Wine Combinations

Pizza, the spicier the better, and Champagne.
(Barbara Fairchild, executive editor, *Bon Appétit*)

A smoky split pea and ham soup, and a rich, smoky French Burgundy.

A cold glass of Gewurztraminer, and a juicy, ripe peach.
(Marie Simmons, cookbook author, N.Y.)

A classic, but I love it: a perfect roast chicken with a grand cru Beaujolais.
(Daniel Johnnes, wine steward, Montrachet, N.Y.)

*Angel-hair pasta with crème fraiche and
a scoop of good caviar on top, with Champagne.*

*A new twist on oyster shooters: Pour the oyster liquid out of fresh oysters
on the half shell, fill with a cold, crisp Sauvignon Blanc, and slurp.*
(Fred Leighton, Bayway World of Liquors, Elizabeth, N.J.)

*Smoked salmon with a dry Riesling: the acidic bite
of the wine contrasts with the ultra-rich silkiness of the smoked salmon.*
(Dorie Greenspan, cookbook author, N.Y.)

*A plate of fresh figs, real Italian prosciutto, good oil-cured olives
and creamy goat cheese, with a Pinot Gris or Sauvignon Blanc with herbaceous,
figgy, melony tastes, and a slightly crisp, citrusy finish.*
(John Sarich, culinary director, Chateau Ste. Michelle Winery, Wash.)

A real Zinfandel, redolent of ripe berries, and a chocolate pot de crème.
(John Scharffenberger, Scharffenberger Cellars, Anderson Valley, Calif.)

Stir-fried pheasant or duck breast with a zesty orange-ginger sauce, and Champagne.
(Susan Spicer, chef, Bayona, New Orleans)

4

A Simple Tasting Strategy

The first time I went to a serious wine tasting, I could barely keep a straight face. Everybody was holding the glasses up and squinting into the light, swirling the wine recklessly and sticking their noses deep within the glasses, swishing as if they had a mouthful of Listerine and then — after all that — spitting it out! It took me more than one tasting to join in, and a few more to go for the gusto. I have to admit, though, that when I got over my embarrassment, I started to see some logic in this silly-looking procedure.

You don't have to squint, swirl, swish and gurgle to enjoy wine. But using the following low-key steps will help you appreciate all the aspects of the wine you drink. Call it the *eyes-nose-mouth method:* look at the wine, smell the wine, and taste the wine. (Actually *drinking* the wine isn't included. Professionals spit it out at competitions and business tastings, though they swallow when they sit down to dinner. Anyway, you don't need any coaching on swallowing.)

Eyes, Nose and Mouth

Here's how to put your senses to full use when you're tasting a wine:

Look at the wine. When you pick up a wine glass, grasp it by the stem — that's what it's there for. You want to be able to see the wine clearly, and you don't want to warm it up by letting the bowl of the glass sit in the palm of

Although color is one of the attributes that wine is judged on, smell and taste are far more important. A blind person can know as much about wine as a sighted person.

The old practice of producing unfiltered wines is coming back as a new trend among smaller artisan winemakers, especially in the United States and France. They believe that the modern habit of filtering wine to make it perfectly clear robs it of flavor and character, and that if wine is handled gently, more of its delicacy and nuance will be preserved. If you see a bottle of wine that seems a bit cloudy, check the label to see if the wine is unfiltered.

your hand. Some wine geeks hold the glass by the base, but that's a bit much.

Hold the glass up to light so you can get a good idea of the wine's color. Wine isn't just white or red. Whites can vary from almost colorless to pale gold to straw-colored to almost amber; sometimes they show flashes of green or pink. Reds can range from pinkish shades to deep ruby or practically purple. Color can give clues about the age of a wine. Older reds often take on a brick tinge and older whites turn gold or deep amber. (While color isn't a foolproof guide to quality, beware if a young wine — say, less than five years old — looks brownish, because it could be spoiled.)

Just as appetizing-looking food seems to taste better than a poorly presented dish, color is an important part of the aesthetic impression a wine makes. A deep ruby-colored wine can seem richer and more flavorful than a pale red one; a pale gold Champagne seems to catch the light and make the dinner table more beautiful.

Take a moment to look at the color and describe it, at least to yourself.

In general, well-made wine should be clear, not cloudy, and there shouldn't be any debris floating around in it. Professional wine tasters rank wines as brilliant, clear, cloudy or murky. With modern wine-making techniques, most of the wines you'll see will be at least clear. Sometimes old wines contain a little harmless sediment.

Smell the wine. Just as almost every rose has its own subtly different and individual scent, so does almost every wine. Good wine smells wonderful. Its fragrance, called the *bouquet* or *nose,* is complicated; you don't have to be an expert to detect a number of different aromas in even the simplest wines. With just a little bit of experience, you may find hints of apple and new-mown grass in a Sauvignon Blanc, or ripe raspberries and black pepper in a Zinfandel.

So, how do you make sure your nose gets the maximum thrill out of a glass of wine? After you've inspected the wine visually, swirl it vigorously around the glass. This is not merely an affectation of wine snobs. In fact, swirling brings more of the wine in contact with air, which releases more of its *esters* — volatile liquids that contain the wine's aromatic qualities. (It's a matter of simple physics. When the wine's sitting flat in the glass, only the top surface, a flat disk, is in contact with air. When you swirl, the disk becomes a cone, and much more wine comes in contact with the air. More air equals more bouquet.)

If a wine is too cold, it won't have much bouquet. Frozen or chilled foods don't have any aroma, and neither does very cold wine. Let the wine warm up. If it still doesn't smell like much then you've just got a wine that doesn't have a very pronounced aroma.

Take a minute or two to enjoy the olfactory treats that the wine has to offer, and identify them if you can. It's not unusual to find the nose changing subtly as more oxygen gets into the wine.

Taste the wine. Take a sip and swish it around your mouth, letting it run all over your tongue. If you want to seem like a real pro — and you're not sitting at the dinner table — suck in some air and gurgle. This seems silly, but, just like swirling, it puts more of the wine in contact with air, and sends those delicious vapors up toward your olfactory bulb, which is behind the top of your nose. (It's the spot where you get a headache when you eat ice cream too fast.) Your sense of smell isn't limited to smelling aromas outside your body, at the tip of your nose; it also constantly samples the air in your mouth.

You may be able to recognize sensations of sweetness and acidity. Does the wine taste thin and acidic? Does it taste too sweet, or is it pleasantly crisp, with acidity balancing out the sweetness or fruitiness?

How does the wine feel in your mouth? Is it smooth and rounded, or tannic — that is, rough and sandpapery? Most red wines are more tannic than most white wines. The acidity in some wines can make you pucker. Others

---

A few of the many scents of wine

Whites
apple, pear, peach, melon, grapefruit, lemon, butter, vanilla, honey, roses, fresh-cut grass, hay, asparagus, bell pepper, vanilla, mint

Reds
blackberry, cherry, raspberry, black pepper, butter, plum, violets, tobacco, smoke, chocolate, mushrooms, wet dirt

Add your own impressions.

"Learning is not an accumulation of knowledge. Learning is movement from moment to moment."

Krishnamurti

can have a tannic astringency that leaves your mouth feeling almost dry.

Think for a moment about whether you like the taste and feel of this wine, and try to describe it to yourself. Then swallow or spit.

The Finish Line

Don't tune out the moment you swallow or spit. Zero in for just a second or two more on what's called the finish — the combination of tastes and sensations that remains in your mouth, like the echo of an organ in a cathedral after the music ends. Some wines reverberate in your mouth for a relatively long time, which draws out the pleasure of drinking them. Some have very little finish, which doesn't necessarily mean they're badly made wines, just that a long finish isn't their style. In any case, the finish should be pleasant and clean-tasting, and shouldn't leave any strange aftertaste.

Congratulations

You've just completed the most important steps on the path to enjoying wine. Just as you can read anything once you've learned to read, so the vocabulary and tasting skills you've learned can apply to any wine (not to mention Kool-Aid and espresso). As you drink wine over time, you'll get better and better at discerning the subtle aromas and tastes, and you'll become more confident about deciding what you like.

> ### How wines can feel in your mouth
>
> silky, smooth, velvety, sharp, big, refreshing, prickly, round, rough, rich, firm, intense, crisp, puckery, lush, creamy, lively, flat
>
> ### Add your own impressions.

Safe Swirling Technique

The key to safe swirling: the glass should be large and no more than half full, preferably only about one-third full. If it's fuller, swirl at your peril, and make sure that you've got spot remover on hand. You can always pour yourself some more wine after you've done your tasting routine.

Holding the glass by the stem, start swirling, perhaps timidly at first but more vigorously as you gain confidence and realize you aren't going to slosh it all over. Many folks do their swirling with the glass still sitting on the table, by grabbing it low on the stem and moving the base flat on the table in a small circular motion. (This works really well on a smooth table surface, but not so well on a tablecloth.) Then they lean over quickly while the wine's still swirling and sniff from the glass, or bring the glass quickly to their nose and breathe deeply.

Beginners may prefer this method to start because it's slightly less risky than freeform high-wire swirling. If you want to practice your technique, pour some water in a wine glass and swirl away.

Favorite Food and Wine Combinations

*Bittersweet chocolate with a full-bodied Rhône wine like Gigondas,
which stands up to the fullness of the chocolate.*
(Veronica Manjarrez, Crown Wine Merchants, Coral Gables, Fla.)

*Grilled salmon, steamed asparagus,
crusty roasted new potatoes, and a fruity, slightly tannic Pinot Noir.*

Sparkling wine with Chinese food.
(Lawrence Solomon, Foremost Sunset Corners, Miami)

Fresh oysters, a few drops of lemon juice, and Pinot Gris.

Dry Riesling with an aged dry Jack cheese and a ripe Comice pear.
(Leslie Cole, writer, Portland, Ore.)

Spicy Thai food with a crisp dry German Riesling.
(Manfred Krankl, Campanile, Los Angeles)

For our Thanksgiving dinner with all the trimmings, the wine is always Zinfandel.
(Marie Simmons, cookbook author, N.Y.)

*Spanish paella, with shrimp, lobster, chicken,
spicy sausage and lots of saffron rice, with a big, oaky Chardonnay.*

Pinot Noir with a duck quesadilla with mole *sauce:
the cinnamon quality of the* mole *goes with the earthy, truffly quality of the wine.*
(Randall Grahm, Bonny Doon Vineyard, Santa Cruz, Calif.)

Orange souffle with vanilla custard sauce and Extra-Dry Champagne.

*Crusty, yeasty sourdough bread
spread with roasted garlic, and a velvety, fruity Pinot Noir.*
(Susan Sokol Blosser, Sokol Blosser Winery, Ore.)

Choosing a Wine

C hoosing a wine is hardly an exact science. Most experienced wine drinkers enjoy many different wines, and base their choices on some nebulous combination of factors, including what's in the cupboard, the food they're about to eat, curiosity about trying something new, what the wine merchant had on special, and perhaps the phase of the moon.

But the most important consideration is definitely the type of grape the wine's made from. More than anything else, *the variety of grape* — also called the *varietal* — determines the flavors, aromas and overall character of the wine.

The wines considered the greatest in the world are made from varietals that originated in Europe. Though thousands of types of grapes exist, only a couple of dozen or so are used to make most fine table wines. Over the centuries, these are the grapes that have proved to make outstanding wines. They are classified botanically as *vitis vinifera,* and wine people refer to the whole category simply as *vinifera.*

Vinifera grapes include Chardonnay, Cabernet Sauvignon, Sauvignon Blanc, Pinot Noir, Chenin Blanc, Merlot and many others. (Many of the grapes originating in North America are classified as *vitis labrusca.* The best known North American variety is Concord, with its classic grape-jelly flavor.)

When a wine is made mostly or completely from one variety of grape, it is called a *varietal-designated wine,* a term which is often shortened to *varietal wine,* or, most commonly, *varietal.* (That's right: the term *varietal* is used two ways, to describe a type of grape and to describe a type of wine.) Calling a wine a varietal sets it apart from low-quality jug wines that mix several grapes. "Hey, dude, this isn't Rotgut Red, it's a varietal, Cabernet Sauvignon!" In 1992, for the first time since records on wine sales have been kept, more than half of all table wines sold in the United States were varietal wines rather than jug wines.

A Variety of Varietals

I'm concentrating especially on some of the varietals grown in France, because most of the grapes grown in the United States are the same ones that are grown in France. Also, most American winemakers have been inspired by the French tradition. Becoming familiar with the grapes grown in France will give you a solid foundation for becoming a smart wine consumer. Eventually, if Spanish, Italian or German wines interest you, you can go on to learn about the particular grapes of those countries.

The list below gives you typical characteristics of each grape and the aromas and flavors associated with it. It's a good starting-point. But drinking wine is a sensual experience, not an intellectual one, and the written description of a sensual experience can never be more than a pathetic substitute for the real thing.

White Wines
Chardonnay

Widely considered the greatest of all white-wine grapes. Used for white Burgundy, the most expensive dry white wines in the world. Generally a light or medium straw color, shading toward gold in older or oak-aged wines. Almost always dry. Typically has buttery and fruity aromas (citrus, especially lemon, peach, pear, apple). Often aged in oak barrels, where it picks up vanilla or toasty flavors. If grown in warm climates (such as California) can be somewhat higher in alcohol than other dry white wines.

Chenin Blanc

Generally pale to medium straw color, sometimes with small glints of green. Grown in California and the Loire Valley of France. Often has honeydew melon, citrus and herbal aromas. In California, usually made in slightly sweet (off-dry) style. Sometimes slightly effervescent.

Gewurztraminer

Aromas of fine Gewurztraminer can be very intense, combining spice (cardamom, nutmeg, cloves) honey, flowers and fruit (especially rose-petal, grapefruit and litchi-nut). Sometimes dry, sometimes slightly sweet. Pale to medium straw color. Beringer 1949

Pinot Gris

Depending on origin, can be remarkably different styles. In Alsace (where it is sometimes labeled Tokay-Pinot Gris), and in Oregon, can be a rich, almost mouth-coating; in Italy, tends to be crisp, dry, one-dimensional in comparison. Light straw color, sometimes a coppery hue. Almost always dry. Notes of citrus, green apple, sometimes a little spice. Lively acidity and pleasant fruitiness make it excellent with food.

Riesling

Also known as White Riesling or, on some California labels, as Johannisberg Riesling (named after the Johannisberg vineyard, greatest of Germany's Riesling vineyards). Best-known versions from Germany and Alsace region of France. Pale to medium straw color. Honey, fruity (citrus, peach, apricot, mint, pineapple), flowery aromas make it seem sweet even when dry. Often off-dry. Good with food because of high acidity and intense fruitiness.

Sauvignon Blanc

Also known as Fumé Blanc in the United States. Almost always dry. Generally straw-colored, sometimes shading toward gold, sometimes toward green. Grassy, leafy, sometimes herbaceous (celery, asparagus, green pepper) aromas; also citrus, flowery, crisp apple and pear.

"It tastes like a little angel is peeing on my tongue."

an old German expression to describe a delicious wine

Very food-friendly wine, lighter in body than Chardonnay, with acidic zing.

Semillon

Light to medium straw color, sometimes with touch of green. Herbaceous or grassy, with lush banana, fig and pepper notes. In white Bordeaux, usually blended with Sauvignon Blanc to soften Sauvignon Blanc's sharp acidity and add rounder flavors. Blend also used in France for unctuously rich, sweet Sauternes dessert wines — Chateau d'Yquem, the most celebrated, can cost hundreds of dollars a bottle. (Don't confuse with cheap domestic "Sauterne.") In the United States, increasingly blended with Chardonnay in delicious, crisp wines.

Red Wines

Cabernet Sauvignon

One of varieties in French Bordeaux, where it is often blended with Merlot, Cabernet Franc or both. Frequently bottled in United States as 100 percent Cabernet Sauvignon. Deep, rich ruby-garnet color, shading toward brick as wines age. When young (less than five years old), tannin can overwhelm fruity qualities, but much depends on winemaker's style. Herbaceous (mint, tea, bell pepper, olives, asparagus, eucalyptus), berry (blackberry, currant, raspberry), vanilla from oak aging.

Gamay

In France, Gamay used for Beaujolais, light, fruity wine, deep pink color, berry and cherry notes. In the United States, a different grape is also called Gamay (sometimes Napa Gamay); U.S. Gamay wines have similar light, fruity style. Drink both American and French versions young.

Merlot

Quickly becoming popular in the United States in varietal wines. Generally a deep ruby color, sometimes almost purple. Fruit (berry, black cherry, plum, spice), tobacco and cedar. Softer, more supple, less tannic than Cabernet Sauvignon; often blended with Cabernet Sauvignon for rounder, softer flavors. Can be delicious young.

Pinot Noir Turning Leaf Coastal Reserve 1999

Considered by some the most sensual and satisfying of all wines. Used for French Burgundy, which can be most expensive of all red wines. Where Merlot and Cabernet Sauvignon are big, forceful and intense, Pinot Noir is delicate and nuanced. Also cultivated successfully in California and Oregon. Ruby color. Fruity (berry, black cherry, wild cherry), sometimes flowery (violet) aromas, notes of cedar, leather, truffles, fresh-turned earth.

Syrah

Still fairly rare as varietal wine on United States shelves. Should become more common, as winemakers take advantage of deep ruby color, moderate tannins, aromas of white pepper, blackberry, licorice and anise. In France, grown in northern Rhône region for celebrated wines Côte-Rôtie and Hermitage. Called Shiraz in Australia.

Zinfandel

Probably found only in the United States. (It may — or may not — have descended from Primitivo, an Italian or Spanish grape variety; speculating on its origins is a common preoccupation of wine nuts.) Can make intense, full-bodied ruby-purple wine, with aromas of raspberry, black pepper and briery smells suggesting a ramble in the underbrush. Picks up vanilla and cedar aromas from aging in oak. Often quite high in alcohol. Also used for the popular slightly sweet White Zinfandel or "blush" wines.

Branching Out

For several years, American wine drinkers have had a love affair with Cabernet Sauvignon and Chardonnay. Both varietals have a long and noble tradition and can make wonderful wine, but I suspect that at least some of

A wine that "goes down as easily as a little Jesus in velvet underpants."

an old Burgundian
expression of approval

their popularity here is due merely to familiarity. People recognize these wines and feel comfortable ordering them. However, popularity has also pushed their prices up, sometimes on the strength of varietal name alone. Cabernet Sauvignon and Chardonnay can be priced far above equally interesting and delicious wines made with lesser-known (in America, at least) grapes.

No matter what you choose, you'll find that wines made with the same grape variety can be quite different, depending on where the grapes were grown and especially on the winemaking style, that is, how the wine was made. Also, though each grape has its own character, even experts can't always distinguish between different red wines or white wines. Someone once asked the British wine authority Harry Waugh if he ever mixed up Bordeaux and Burgundy, two French reds made with different grapes. "Not since lunch," Waugh replied.

6

Name That Wine:
Understanding the Logic of Labels

A friend of mine learned to love Beaujolais on her first trip to France, one of those great college backpacking jaunts. When she came home to the United States, she went right out and bought a jug of a California red wine labeled Beaujolais — and was disappointed to discover that it was nothing like the delightful French wine she remembered.

My friend had fallen into the gap between the Old World and the New World. She didn't know that, as a general rule, French regional names like Beaujolais, Chablis or Burgundy on American wines are likely to have little connection to the originals. Laws in California and some other states allow winemakers to use French names for wines that don't have the slightest resemblance to the French originals. The grapes don't even have to be the same.

In most cases, a wine is primarily named on the label in one of two ways:

- **by varietal (variety of grape)**

- **by geographical origin (where the wine is from)**

Why not both? In one word: tradition.
In the Old World, as the cultivation of wine grapes evolved over the

Pronouncing Varietal Names

I once met a Dutch truck driver who spoke five languages. I envied him. At the time, I was struggling along learning my first foreign language, and it wasn't easy. Of course, after I thought about it for a while, I realized that this guy had been on the road for years, driving to Germany and France and Italy and Spain. He'd been reading road signs, doing business, picking up girls, eating in restaurants. No wonder he could speak all those languages; he'd had years of practice.

Learning to pronounce the names of the varietals is nowhere near as tough as learning a whole new language, and the more you do it, the easier it gets. Here are a few of the most common ones.

Red Wines

Cabernet Sauvignon ....CAB-er-nay SO-veen-yawn
(but many people just call it "Cab")

Merlot..Mer-LO

Pinot Noir ....PEE-no nwar

Zinfandel..ZIN-fan-del

Syrah ....Sir-RAH

White Wines

Sauvignon Blanc...SO-veen-yawn BLAHNK

Pinot Gris ....PEE-no gree

Riesling..REES-ling

Gewurztraminer ....Ge-VURTZ-tra-mee-ner
(sometimes shortened to Ge-VURTZ)

Semillon...SEM-mee-yawn

Chardonnay...CHAR-don-nay

As for pronouncing the names of the thousands of wineries, villages and regions in French, Italian, German and Spanish, try this: fearlessly ask how things are pronounced when you buy them in restaurants and wine shops, and plunge right in. I've often heard wine people mispronounce foreign names, and I've done a good share of it myself.

centuries, farmers noticed that certain varieties seemed best suited to certain regions. A particular grape grew better in certain places, developed better flavors and made better wine. Eventually, some grapes and geographical locations became so closely associated that they were almost synonymous, and wines became known by their region.

Bordeaux, Chablis, Burgundy, Beaujolais: each is a region in France, and each is associated with particular grape varieties. Wines from much of Europe are labeled with the region (and sometimes the village and even the vineyard) where they're grown. I remember the flash of recognition on my first trip to Burgundy when I looked at a map and realized that the names of all the little villages along the highway were the same as the labels I had been looking at on wine lists!

In France, government regulations require wines from certain regions to be made with certain grapes only, and only wines made in a given region can carry that region's name. Some regions, like Beaujolais, are huge, and have smaller sub-regions within them, all governed by the same exacting regulations.

Specific wine-growing regions in France are called *appellations d'origine controlées* (literally, "designation of inspected origin"). They're usually referred to as simply *appellations controlées* (pronounced ap-pel-la-see-OWN control-AY) or sometimes by the initials A.O.C. A wine label might read *Appellation Pauillac* [the name of the region] *Controlée* or *Appellation Bandol Controlée*

> *Thank heaven for the Alsatians! Taking a cue from their German ancestors rather than their French winemaking counterparts, they label their wines with the name of the varietal, as well as its geographical origin. This means you can more easily find an Alsatian wine, like a Riesling, Gewurztraminer or Pinot Gris, that's similar to an American wine you've enjoyed.*

In the New World, Labels Are Different

In the New World — including the United States, Canada, South America, Australia, New Zealand and South Africa — wines are primarily labeled by varietal, not geographical origin. We don't have a long tradition of raising only certain grapes in certain regions, so geographical labels alone would be useless to the consumer who wanted to know what sort of wine was in the bottle.

Geography's still important, though. Almost all American wines carry their geographical origin on the label. You'll see wines marked Napa Valley or Mendocino County or simply New York or Washington. Sometimes, if a wine comes from an area that's developed a reputation for making particularly good wine — like Carneros or Howell Mountain in the Napa Valley — you'll see that specified as well.

The key difference is that, if you see a bottle of French wine labeled Chablis, you'll know exactly what grape the wine was made from. (It's Chardonnay, by the way.) In the United States, the name of an American region on a wine label will not tell you precisely what grape variety is in the bottle.

Name's Different, Grape's the Same

In the United States, geographical divisions called American Viticultural Areas, or AVA's, are the closest United States equivalent to the French appellations controlées. The AVA's define the boundaries of some distinctive wine-growing areas and guarantee that most or all of the wine in the bottle is grown in the area specified, but they do not guarantee that a wine is made from a particular grape.

If you're looking for American wines that resemble French favorites — or vice versa — you need to know which varieties are grown in which French regions. For example, in Burgundy, white wines are always made from Chardonnay and red wines from Pinot Noir; in Bordeaux reds, the principal ingredient is either Cabernet Sauvignon or Merlot. If you love Merlot, you might try some Bordeaux from the Pomerol region, where Merlot is a principal ingredient. If you see a white Bordeaux on the wine shop shelf, you'll know that there's Sauvignon Blanc and Semillon in the bottle.

In a restaurant, when the waiter says, "I recommend a nice Pouilly-Fuissé" or "We've got a terrific Nuits St.-Georges on special this week," don't hesitate to ask what grape the wine is made from. It's a perfectly reasonable question. (The first is a white wine, the second's red, both are from Burgundy, so the answers will be Chardonnay and Pinot Noir.) An American or Australian Chardonnay won't be exactly like a French one, but knowing the grape should give you at least a general idea of the characteristics of the wine.

The chart that follows lists some of the most common New World-Old World equivalents. You don't have to memorize it, although you might want to pay special attention to a few of your favorites.

Matching the New World with the Old World

New World by grape variety	**Old World** by geographic origin

Red Wines

Cabernet Sauvignon ....Bordeaux, including Pauillac, St.-Julien, Margaux and Médoc districts

Merlot..............................Bordeaux, especially Pomerol and St.-Emilion districts

Pinot Noir ....Burgundy

Syrah ....Northern Rhône Valley wines, like Côte-Rôtie, Hermitage, St.-Joseph, Cornas

Grenache..Southern Rhône Valley wines, like Châteauneuf-du-Pape, Côtes du Rhône (often blended with Syrah, Mourvèdre and others)

Cabernet Franc ....Chinon, Bourgueil

Sangiovese (Italy)..Chianti

Nebbiolo (Italy)..Barolo, Barbaresco

White Wines

Sauvignon Blanc and Semillon (blended) ....Bordeaux, especially Graves Sauternes (sweet white dessert wines)

Chardonnay ....Chablis, Burgundy, including Meursault, Pouilly-Fuissé, Puligny-Montrachet

Sauvignon Blanc (unblended) ....Pouilly-Fumé, Sancerre

Chenin Blanc ....Vouvray, Savennières

Neither Here nor There

To complicate matters, winemakers can give their wines unique names that reflect neither geographic origin nor the type of grape in the bottle. Some do it for marketing purposes, others for romance, superstition or sheer whimsy. Wines with such names are called *proprietary wines.*

In some cases, the winemakers are required, by law, to come up with an unusual name; in California, for example, the law allows a wine to be labeled with a varietal name only if at least 75 percent of the wine is made from that grape. (Other states have similar regulations.) If a wine has smaller percentages of several grapes, then it can't have a varietal name on the label.

Among the world's proprietary names, perhaps the most famous is Mouton Cadet, the "junior" (that's *cadet* in French) label from Bordeaux's famed Chateau Mouton-Rothschild. Other examples, on a much smaller scale, are Quintet, a blend of five grapes from William Wheeler Winery, and Conundrum, a white wine made of four different grapes, from Caymus Vineyards. Trefethen Vineyards is known for its Eschol wines. One of my favorite proprietary names is Grateful Red, a Pinot Noir from Redhawk Vineyards in Oregon.

You may see a category called Meritage (rhymes with *heritage*) on wine lists. That's a newly invented word for Bordeaux-style blends made in California. Since many of the Meritage wines include less than 75 percent of any one grape, winemakers got together and came up with a classy-sounding name for their aspiring Bordeaux.

Like French Bordeaux, the reds are made primarily of Cabernet Sauvignon and Merlot. White Meritage wines, following the French tradition, are made mostly of Sauvignon Blanc and Semillon. Each separate wine within the group has its own name; the best-known is Opus One.

Why does Bordeaux end in an "x"? And, for that matter, why is it spelled the same way whether it's singular or plural?

Bordeaux is the name of the region which gives its name to the wines. And, since those wacky French sometimes make plurals by adding an "x" to words, and French words often sound the same whether they're singular or plural, English-speaking writers seem to have agreed to just say Bordeaux, whether they mean the place, one bottle of Bordeaux or twenty bottles of Bordeaux.

Anyway, Bordeauxs looks really odd.

Over the next few years, it's possible the definition of Meritage will expand to include high-quality blended wines that are not made from Bordeaux varietals.

American wine lovers have developed the habit of buying varietal wines, but nothing guarantees that those are necessarily the best or most delicious wines. Wines blended from several grapes can be more complex and better-tasting than single-grape wines. Another advantage is that they're often less expensive than varietal-designated wines. Blended wines have made the reputations of some winemakers, notably Randall Grahm of Bonny Doon Vineyard in California's Santa Cruz Mountains. Grahm's fancifully named wines, inspired by the wines of the Rhône Valley in southern France, include Le Cigare Volant (which means Flying Cigar, the French name for a UFO), and Old Telegram (homage to a legendary French wine called Vieux Télégraphe).

Proprietary wines can be tricky to get to know, because the names don't fit into established categories — but, on the plus side, they're easy to remember once you try them, because the names are so distinctive, and sometimes downright funny. Who could forget Refrigerator White, made in Sonoma County by winemaker and perennial presidential candidate Pat Paulsen? When you see a wine with an unusual name, read the label to get some clues about what's in the bottle.

> To appeal to varietal-conscious American consumers, some wine producers in the south of France are using varietal names on their labels. The wines are usually inexpensive, and some are good values. But you won't see varietal labels replacing the chateaux and geographical names of the great French wines.

Bordeaux

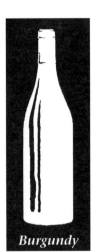

Burgundy

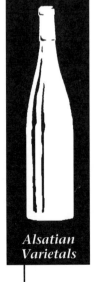

Alsatian
Varietals

The Secret's in the Shape

The shape of a wine bottle can tell you what type of wine is inside. Traditionally, certain shapes are associated with certain regions of France. French Bordeaux, both red and white, come in bottles with "shoulders." Burgundy bottles have sloping sides. Many Alsatian wines, like Riesling and Gewurztraminer, are bottled in tall, skinny bottles.

The bottles used by New World wine-growing regions usually follow France's lead for the same grape varieties. Bordeaux grapes show up in the same type of bottle as Bordeaux. A Washington State Chardonnay usually comes in the same sort of bottle as a white French Burgundy, because they're made from the same grape. An Oregon Riesling will frequently look just like an Alsatian Riesling, in a long-necked bottle that's often made of brown glass rather than green.

7

Easy Ways
to Train Your Taste Buds

A true story: Three successful professional women are having dinner
together to discuss the purchase of an office building. Perceptive
comments about break-even points, interest rates, cash-on-cash returns and
depreciation schedules fly around the table. But then the wine list arrives.

The conversation stalls.

"Oh, I don't know, I think I want something sweet," says one.

"I really only drink white wines," says another.

They hand the list to the third member of the party, my friend Jo.
"You choose," they tell her.

Jo, who wouldn't call herself a wine expert but knows what she likes,
plunges right in and orders a Merlot, which is definitely not sweet and
definitely not white. "They both loved it," she reports.

Obviously, Jo's companions hadn't ever paid much attention to the
wines they were served. They had a couple of notions about what they liked
— mistaken notions, as it turned out. Thanks to Jo's initiative, they were
exposed to something new, and they liked it a lot.

The "exercises" below are really just ways of adding a wine focus to
situations you're going to be in anyway. They'll help you identify the
differences between varietals, zero in on what you like, and painlessly
expand your horizons.

Painless Way #1

As with food, you can learn more about what you like — about what just plain tastes better to you — by comparing two different wines simultaneously.

• If you'll need two bottles of wine for a dinner party, don't buy two of the same thing. Buy different wines, open them at the same time, and serve them side by side. Taste and compare. Which do you like better?

• Try buying the same varietal from two different wineries, two different regions or even two different countries, like an Alsatian Pinot Gris and a Pinot Grigio from Italy.

• Go for two different varietals of the same color, say, a Pinot Noir and a Zinfandel. Don't know if you prefer Merlot or Cabernet Sauvignon? Buy a bottle of each. For a more subtle comparison, buy the same varietal from two different vintages, countries, or wineries.

Painless Way #2

• If you're ordering wine by the glass at a restaurant, turn what is usually mindless sipping into a learning experience. Convince each of your companions to order a different wine. Remember which one is which, or hang onto the menu or wine list to keep them straight. Then taste around and decide which ones you like best. (Ask for big enough glasses to do some swirling, and don't bother to do this with anonymous "house" wines.)

• If the restaurant offers half-bottles on the wine list, order two different half-bottles rather than one full-sized bottle.

Painless Way #3

• After you've been paying attention to wine for a while, buy some inexpensive jug wine — you know, the stuff you can find at any supermarket. Taste it with full attention, and describe it carefully. Do you like it? If you do, that's OK — jug wines are not necessarily bad, but they're usually not very interesting. Now that you've tried some other wines, see how they compare.

• Just for fun, pour the jug wine into one carafe or pitcher and a varietal wine into another. See, smell and savor. Can you tell which is which? Which one do you prefer?

Painless Way #4

• If your local wine shop has tastings — especially free tastings — take advantage of them. But don't just sniff and slurp in your own little corner. Talk with the proprietor and your fellow shoppers about what you're tasting.

• Ask what sort of foods would go with the wine, or what makes a certain winery's products stand out. Wine people love to talk about wine. You're sure to get into some interesting conversations, and learn something, too.

Painless Way #5

• Next time you're having dinner with a companion, pour two glasses of wine, but don't drink right away. Taste the wine, then describe it to your friend, using as many of the senses as possible. What color is it, precisely? What aromas are there? How does it feel in the mouth? Then have your companion taste the same wine. Does he or she agree with your description, or have other reactions?

• After twenty minutes or a half hour, taste and describe the wine again. Has it changed? How? Many wines change noticeably after they've been exposed to air for a while.

• For a variation, use two different wines and describe them to each other.

Coffee, Tea . . . or Gewurztraminer?

If you're trying to figure out where to start with wine, take a tip from veteran wine steward Joseph Nase.

To help customers figure out what types of wine they'd like, he asks about other drinks they enjoy.

"Do you like your coffee or tea with sugar? Are sweet soft drinks like cola your favorites? When you order a mixed drink, is it something like a daiquiri or a Manhattan? In that case, you might not want to plunge right into completely dry or very acidic wines," says Nase. "Your taste buds probably are accustomed to a bit of sweetness."

Nase advises people in this category to ask for wines that are off-dry. White wines like Riesling, Chenin Blanc and Gewurztraminer are often made in a slightly sweet style. (Don't ask for a "sweet wine," though, or you'll get something intended to be enjoyed with dessert.) You may want to move on to drier wines eventually, but your palate first needs some time to make the transition.

On the other hand, let's say you drink scotch, vodka or mineral water, and prefer your coffee unsweetened. Then your palate is probably prepared for dry wines. However, few people start right off drinking very dry or tannic wines. A little sugar takes the edge off some of wine's more difficult qualities, and eventually you may start to enjoy drier wines — or you may not.

The Final Exam

Look at these three wine descriptions, from three different magazines:

" . . . gorgeous perfumed aromas with delicious cherry and raspberry fruit in the mouth, and . . . a terrific lingering finish of cinnamon, nutmeg and truffles."

" . . . moderately intense . . . aromas [of] cherry, tobacco, leather. . . Nice blackberry flavors integrated well with clove."

"Herb, smoke and meat aromas with some chocolate. Deep, ripe spiced cherry fruit and herb flavors are long, lush and forward."

Sound like three beautiful wines, don't they? Would you believe that they're all descriptions of Pinot Noir? What's more, they all describe the exact same wine!

And that's exactly the point. Tasting wine is a subjective experience, and what matters most is what you think, and what you like. In this case, three experienced tasters drinking the same wine give us three descriptions that overlap in some ways, and seem very different in others. Two reviewers mention herb flavors, and all three mention cherry. But one finds tobacco where the other senses truffles, and one smells smoke where the other smells fire — I mean, leather.

The most important thing is that they all like the wine very much. They've tasted carefully and with full attention. They have the vocabulary to describe what they've tasted. And they've got the confidence to say, "Yes, I like this."

"There ain't no answer. There ain't going to be any answer. There never has been an answer. That's the answer."

Gertrude Stein

Women and Wine

Women do not have a monopoly on feeling uncomfortable about wine, but they do have a couple of strikes against them. For a very long time, the world of wine was almost exclusively male, and it has only recently begun to change. For many years, women were not even accepted for training as winemakers. Female wine stewards were unheard-of. Some wine appreciation classes enrolled only men, and the prestigious food and wine societies were male-only bastions. Even today, few published wine "authorities" are female. More important, from an individual consumer's point of view, our society's image of a connoisseur who had mastered the intricacies of wine was exclusively male.

Nowadays, there's a small but growing likelihood that the wine steward at your table or the wine merchant at the corner store will be female. Women can join the top food and wine societies, although they remain in the minority. And women winemakers are crafting some of the world's most respected wines. In fact, some biological research shows that women in general have more acute senses of taste and smell than men, and so may be better suited physiologically for making wine and evaluating it.

Opening Wine Like a Pro

Well, world, I'll admit it. I've had my share of moments I'd rather forget trying to open wine bottles. I've broken off some corks, pushed others into the bottle in frustration, and staged a few unseemly tugs-of-war while grasping the bottle delicately between my thighs (very delicately, indeed, when the wine in question is chilled to 45 degrees or thereabouts). Finally, I realized that this was not going to impress the guests. There had to be a better way.

Yes, you can open a bottle and hang onto your dignity simultaneously, and you don't need to limit yourself to wine with twist-off caps to do it. My personal savior is a surpassingly simple corkscrew called the *Screwpull*. You simply screw it in and keep turning, and it eases the cork right out of the bottle. No brute force necessary. And it's got a great non-stick coating, so it just glides into that old cork.

In addition to the Screwpull, two other simple-to-use corkscrews are the *winglever* (the wings go up as you screw it in, then you press them down and the cork lifts out) and the *butler's friend* (the prongs slip in and grip the cork on either side and then you pull it out).

Screwpull

Step-by-Step Instructions

Those who are more mechanically inclined, or who want to emulate flashy wine stewards, gravitate toward the *bootlever* corkscrew, the kind used in most restaurants. It folds up like a jackknife, and has four parts: the corkscrew itself, a lever to wedge against the lip of the bottle, a handle, and a knife for cutting the capsule, the piece of colored plastic or metal that covers the top of the bottle.

Butler's Friend

Using the bootlever properly takes a little practice, however. Have a corkscrew and a bottle of wine in hand as you read the instructions below, then reward yourself with a nice glass of wine when you finish.

Bootlever

1. You'll need some leverage to open the bottle. Either set the bottle on a table and stand up, or hold the bottle below chest height.

2. Wipe the top of the bottle with a napkin or towel, to make sure it's clean. Then, using the knife, cut the capsule. Some people cut the capsule at the very top of the bottle, while others find it easier to cut it lower down, at the second lip of the bottle, because then you can press the knife blade against the neck of the bottle to get a clean cut. There's also less chance of the knife skittering across the top of the bottle and slicing off part of your hand.

Winglever

At home, you can simplify things by removing the capsule completely, but some people think the bottle looks naked without a collar. The capsule often has some writing or decoration on it that adds to the picture the bottle makes on your table.

3. Wipe off the cork if it's dusty or moldy. A little mold or sediment does not mean the wine is spoiled.

4. Hold the corkscrew at an angle, so that the tip points straight down. Insert it into the cork, turn once or twice, then pull the corkscrew straight up to vertical, so it enters straight into the cork. If you're not careful, you will screw the corkscrew into the cork at an angle, which is bad, because it's hard to pull out the cork if the corkscrew's in crooked.

5. The lever has two little hooks on the end. When the corkscrew is in far enough in to allow it, position those over the lip of the bottle. Stop screwing before the corkscrew pierces the bottom of the cork.

6. Grasp the handle and start to lift the cork straight out, using the lever against the rim of the bottle for leverage. Once the leverage is exhausted, keep pulling straight out. Don't pull sideways, because you'll probably break the cork. If pulling on the handle isn't easy, just wrap your hand around the exposed cork and pull straight up.

7. Check the neck for sediment (in red wine) or crystals of tartaric acid (usually found in white wine). Neither means that there's anything wrong with the wine, but, for aesthetic reasons, you can wipe them out with a finger wrapped in a paper towel or napkin. If the occasion is more high-toned, wrap a chopstick in a paper towel and use it like a Q-tip to clean the neck.

Capsule Summary

The latest change in wine bottles is the capsule — the piece of plastic or metal that covers the end of the bottle and protects the top of the cork. Capsules have long been made of lead, a soft, pliable metal which seemed perfect for the job. However, recent discoveries about the dangers of even small amounts of lead in food and drink have prompted some states to ban lead capsules entirely. Many wineries now use plastic, which looks perfectly OK and carries no conceivable health risks. (Some wineries also are experimenting with tin capsules, the scourge of

"During the eighteenth and nineteenth centuries, every well-born gentleman tried his hand at inventing a new corkscrew."

Patrick Dunne, owner of Lucullus, a culinary antique shop, in New Orleans

waiters everywhere, because they're razor-sharp and can easily slice fingers.)

Scientific opinion is not unanimous on whether lead capsules add any lead to wine. But, for safety's sake, if you're drinking from a bottle with a lead capsule, take the capsule off completely (or at least slice it down low enough that the wine won't flow over the metal when pouring), and wipe the lip and inside of the bottle carefully with a damp cloth before you pour.

The Miracle of the Helix

During the 1940s, wine writer Leon D. Adams and physicist Leonard B. Loeb undertook a two-year project testing corkscrews to find out, once and for all, which worked

Helix

best. (I suspect a few good bottles of wine got drunk in the process. After all, they were open, weren't they?) Intrepid investigators Adams and Loeb discovered something of elemental importance about corkscrews: that the "worm" — the screw of the corkscrew — should be a helix, "with point and spirals in perfect alignment . . . which worms its way into the cork without weakening it, and when

Auger

it is pulled, grips the cork from the inside and doesn't let go," Adams writes. Unfortunately, many corkscrews — even five decades after this pioneering research! — are made with sharp-edged augers, which simply dig a hole in the cork and can cause it to disintegrate.

9

Serving It, Storing It, and Knowing When It's "Corked"

Conventional wisdom says that white wines are supposed to be served chilled, and red wines at room temperature. That's not a bad generalization, but it needs a little fine-tuning.

White wine is usually best at a temperature cool enough to bring out the wine's acidity and fruitiness, but not so cold that the bouquet disappears and the wine loses its character. Most people simply serve white wine straight out of the refrigerator, which is usually around 40 degrees. Experts say that it should be served at 55 degrees, but obviously wine won't stay at a constant temperature once it's out of the fridge. If, after you pour, you find the bouquet is very faint or nonexistent, the wine may be too cold. After a few minutes, it should warm up a bit, and the nose may be more apparent. (If it still doesn't smell like much, the wine may just not have much bouquet.)

In general, the sweeter the wine, the cooler it should be served. Cold's tendency to emphasize acidity helps balance the sugar in sweeter wines — say, an off-dry Riesling, Gewurztraminer or Chenin Blanc, or a late-harvest dessert wine. Sparkling wines taste best straight out of the fridge, and should be kept in an ice bucket if they're sitting out for any length of time.

Red wines can be drunk as cool as 55 degrees, but experts agree that most great reds — Cabernet Sauvignon, Merlot, Bordeaux, Chianti Classico, Burgundy and Barolo, to name a few — taste best between 60 and 65 degrees.

A bottle of wine at normal room temperature — say, 68 to 74 degrees — will chill approximately 10 degrees in an hour in a cold refrigerator. To chill it quickly, just put it in the freezer for 10 minutes or so, but don't forget it's there or you'll have a messy illustration of how liquids expand when they freeze.

Fruity, lighter reds, which are mostly designed to be drunk young — Beaujolais, light-styled Pinot Noir, Bardolino and Dolcetto, for example — benefit from a little chilling. Also, the higher percentage of alcohol a wine has, the cooler you want to serve it, to bring out the fruitiness and minimize the "hotness" of the alcohol. Some examples of relatively high-alcohol wines are Barolo, some Burgundy and Châteauneuf-du-Pape, from the southern part of the Rhône Valley.

It's easy to determine your own preferences. Just chill wines in the refrigerator and pour them while they're cold. Keep tasting as they warm up; they change character with the temperature. I tend to prefer red wines a little colder than most people, but you can taste for yourself.

When a red wine is too warm, you'll notice that you're tasting tannin and alcohol, not fruit. If a red wine tastes "hot" or bitter to you, or if it isn't as fruity as you think it should be, don't be afraid to put it in the fridge for a little while. If you're in a restaurant, ask for an ice bucket to chill it down a bit, but be ready to be treated as though you've just asked the waiter to perform a striptease at the table — most waiters seem to think that a red wine should never be cooled, no matter how warm it is. (They're wrong.)

What about the old adage that red wine should be served at room temperature? Well, that made sense when the room in question was in a drafty, ill-heated old stone chateau that probably never got warmer than 65 degrees. But no wines will show off to advantage at 70 degrees or warmer, the typical temperature in a modern home or restaurant.

Typically, wine poured into your glass will warm up at the rate of about one degree every four minutes or so. That's a good reason to chill wines a little colder than their ideal serving temperature.

You needn't become a maniac with a thermometer to get wine to the right temperature range; a little experience and a little tasting, and the wine itself will tell you everything you need to know.

Does Wine Have Lungs?

When a Hollywood screenwriter wants to sum up an insufferable wine snob in just one line, the line is usually: "This wine needs time to breathe." (You supply the vaguely Continental accent.) Yet, even though it sounds silly, there's some useful truth in the idea for anyone interested in wine. Indeed, wines do "breathe."

Air — oxygen, actually — affects wine. Wine needs to come in contact with at least a little air to release its bouquet. Technically, the air causes the esters — fragrant liquids — in wine to evaporate or volatilize. That's why you swirl a wine in your glass before you smell it, and why you get a renewed blast of bouquet every time you swirl again. That's also why a good wine glass is large and tilts gently in at the rim, so it can capture those scents before they float away forever.

A wine will often change in taste as it stands in your glass during the course of a meal, due largely to the effects of air. Most good wines remain tasty over several hours, and part of the pleasure of drinking them is noticing the changes. It's not unusual for one set of flavors to come to the fore when you first pour a wine, and for others to become evident after twenty minutes or so. A wine that you've left open overnight will probably taste very different from the way it did just after you pulled the cork.

Now, what about your wine-loving pal who opens a bottle and then insists on letting it stand on the sideboard for an hour or two? Under those circumstances only a small amount of the wine in the bottle has contact with air — just a circle about the size of a nickel, or the neck of the bottle. The wine is interacting with air, but very, very slowly, probably with little perceptible effect. You would add much more air to the wine by swirling it in your glass.

Demonstrate the effect of oxygen on wine for yourself. For the most obvious results, use a bottle of red wine like Cabernet Sauvignon or Merlot. Open a bottle and pour a small glass of wine. Smell and taste the wine in the glass every half hour or so, and see if it changes. After a few hours, pour another glass from the bottle and compare its

"volatile: 1. passing through the air on wings . . . 2. easily passing off by evaporation: readily vaporizable at a relatively low temperature . . . 3 . . . easily aroused or moved: easily affected by circumstances . . . "

From Webster's
Third New International Dictionary

To store wine longer than a couple of days, researchers have had great results with freezing it. Be sure there's plenty of room in the bottle for expansion. (You may want to freeze it without the cork in the bottle, just in case.)

taste to the wine that's been standing in the first glass you poured.

Some wine lovers take this "breathing" deal to extremes, tasting the wine immediately at opening and then off and on for a day or even two, trying to find some mythical peak moment. For practical purposes, however (not to mention having the wine around to enjoy with your dinner and keeping it at a good serving temperature) your best bet is just to open the bottle and pour the wine right away, swirling and sniffing as you drink.

Storing Leftover Wine

Wine has four enemies — oxygen, heat, light and intense vibration. Once you've opened a bottle and drunk some wine, you've already exposed the contents to oxygen, and probably to two of the other three. Few wines will taste as good the second or third day after you've opened them as they were at first, but they can still be a pleasure to drink, especially if you can minimize the damage.

The simplest way to store leftover wine is to pour it into a clean, empty half-bottle (375 ml), cork it tightly and refrigerate. I always save a few half-bottles, carefully washed, for just this situation. If the bottle is mostly filled with wine, there will be little room remaining for air. Try to avoid laying the bottle on its side in the fridge; if the wine touches the cork, it could pick up some off-flavors, especially if (like me) you've chosen the cork at random from a collection of miscellaneous corks in a drawer.

For longer storage, I've had success with a system called Private Preserve. It's a mixture of three inert gases -- nitrogen, carbon dioxide and argon -- that you shoot into a half-empty wine bottle. The gases, which form a blanket on the surface of the wine to protect against oxidation, preserve aromas and flavors beautifully. You can also use Private Preserve to protect any other liquid that could be harmed by oxidation, like port, sherry, cognac, expensive olive oil or fine vinegar.

Big is Beautiful, or Glassware Made Easy

If you consider what's important in wine tasting, the requirements for the perfect wine glass become obvious.

- Clear glass is the best material, to best appreciate the wine's color.

- A sizeable goblet, at least twelve ounces or even larger, allows vigorous swirling to release the wine's bouquet without spilling.

- A glass that curves in very slightly at the rim helps concentrate the bouquet.

- Ideally, the glass or crystal should be thin, and the rim of the glass (called the *bead)* should not be any thicker than the glass itself.

You needn't worry about things like "red wine glasses" and "white wine glasses." A good, all-purpose glass will do the trick. Shopping carefully, you shouldn't have to spend more than $5 to $8 per glass.

It doesn't matter how wonderful the wine you're drinking is if your glass isn't clean. At home, wipe out glasses carefully before using them. At restaurants, always look at your wine glass carefully to make sure it's clean. Then take a discreet sniff at the empty glass before you let anyone pour anything into it. If the glass smells like detergent, or has a musty odor from being stored upside-down, ask for a clean one. Such odors can interfere with enjoying the wine.

In many restaurants, wine glasses are too small to swirl the wine easily, or at all. What's more, when you order wine by the glass in most places, the bartender usually fills the glass to the brim, probably to head off complaints from folks who think they're getting shortchanged. If you're tempted to react that way, you should know that, in some states, a "glass" of wine is required by law to be a certain minimum amount, usually five or six ounces. That doesn't change whether the wine is forced into a tiny glass or allowed to spread out and blossom in a generous goblet.

See for yourself what different glasses can do. Next time you open a bottle of wine, pour it into several differently shaped glasses and compare the way the wine tastes, and especially how much you can enjoy the bouquet. For a real shock, try drinking the same wine out of one of those plastic glasses people use at parties.

The best glasses for Champagne are flutes or tulips. Tall and skinny, they show off the bubbles.

No matter where you are, a full-to-the-brim glass makes properly appreciating the wine all but impossible. Consider yourself lucky when you receive a large glass half filled rather than a small glass brimming over — because that means you've got room for swirling and sniffing.

What to do when your cup runneth over? Start by asking if the restaurant has any bigger wine glasses. Ask for the biggest glasses you can get, regardless of what color wine they're supposed to be used for.

Some restaurants have a few better glasses that they won't subject to the daily wear-and-tear, but will bring out on request. At dinner not long ago in a restaurant with an impressive wine list, I decided to treat myself to a $30 bottle of Merlot to go with rare prime rib. When the wine came, it seemed wonderful, but the wine glasses were barely the size of billiard balls. Even a mouthful of wine would have sloshed out during an enthusiastic swirl. I asked if there were bigger glasses. "Oh yes, we've got a set of twelve," said the wine steward cheerfully. "We bring them out when someone orders a really good wine."

I let her know that the wine we'd ordered was indeed a "really good" wine, and got the glasses we wanted. You're entitled to do that too, no matter how much — or how little — you spend on wine.

Many serious wine lovers swear by the huge crystal goblets made by Riedel, an Austrian company. They come in several different shapes designed for different wines, although many people have found the Burgundy or Bordeaux glasses to be splendid for drinking just about anything. "Good glasses are a fabulous investment," says one winemaker. "They can make all the difference. It's far cheaper to buy expensive glasses than expensive wine."

As a last resort, if you can't get a bigger wine glass, ask your waiter for what is called in the trade a "rocks" glass or "bucket," the sort of glass a scotch on the rocks would come in, and pour the wine into it. You'll enjoy the wine more, and that's far more important than whether your glass looks right.

And, please, be nice to your waiter if the wine glasses are too small. It's not his fault. The true culprits are restaurant owners who don't care enough about wine to invest in (slightly) more expensive glassware.

When Wine is Spoiled

Wine is a food, and, like all food (with the possible exception of Twinkies and beef jerky), it is perishable. Once in a while, you'll encounter a bottle that's simply not good, perhaps because it's got a bad cork or has been abused in storage.

You usually don't even need to taste a spoiled wine; you'll smell it. A normal reaction on smelling a nice, healthy wine is "aaaaah." If you find yourself saying "yuck" instead, the wine is probably spoiled, often called corked because bad corks are one of the main causes of spoiled wine.

Cork has been used as a stopper for wine bottles for centuries, but many winemakers say the quality of corks has plummeted in recent years, and that perhaps as many as seven to ten percent of corks are faulty. (What exactly makes a cork bad is a controversy that preoccupies the wine world. The latest theory is that a bad cork contains an imperceptible vein of mold which ruins the wine.)

When a cork is bad, the wine can develop "off" odors and tastes. How can you tell? The more experience you have tasting wines, the more confident you'll be about deciding when one is not fit to drink. However, as a general rule, wine, especially young wine, should smell pleasant, fresh, grapey or fruity, sometimes with a hint of oak. If a wine smells unpleasant — like cardboard, mold, wet wood, nail polish or the bottom of your laundry hamper — you've got a bad bottle on your hands.

If you're in a restaurant, politely bring the waiter or wine steward over and tell her that you think the wine is corked. She will probably take a whiff and agree with you, and whisk the offending bottle away. If you've bought the wine from a wine merchant, put the cork back in the bottle and return it; most reputable merchants will give you a refund or a replacement.

But don't jump to conclusions! Some wines give off an unpleasant smell — usually sulphurous, like rotten eggs — in the first few minutes after they're opened. This smell should dissipate or *blow off*, as it's called. So, if you detect a

A bit of mold on the top of a cork or under a capsule doesn't mean a wine is spoiled. Just wipe the mold off carefully with a damp cloth before opening the bottle.

53

Just using the word "corked " to describe a spoiled wine will give you credibility with waiters.

rotten-egg odor, swirl the wine vigorously in your glass to give it a chance to breathe for a short while. Only if the smell persists should you signal the waiter, or return the bottle to the wine merchant. If you have any questions about the way a wine smells, don't hesitate to ask.

In older wines, you're likely to encounter aromas that you haven't smelled in younger ones, which can make it harder to identify a spoiled bottle. Older red wines develop highly prized scents that are often described as rubber, chocolate, burnt toast or tobacco. But appreciating these is an acquired taste, and distinguishing "burnt toast" from "bad wine" can be tough without a lot of experience. If you want to splurge on an older wine, stick to a restaurant with a fine cellar and a wine steward whom you've gotten to know and trust, so you'll have a better chance of getting a wine in good condition.

Though people often describe spoiled wine as "vinegar," good vinegar tastes much better than bad wine. A spoiled wine is often more musty-tasting than vinegary.

10

Wine and Food:
Made for Each Other

W ine without food is incomplete. It's like a bride without a groom, a
senator without a lobbyist, Lucy without Ricky. Though much
"tasting" is done with wine alone, wine comes to life in partnership with a
meal. A wine that tastes thin and acidic by itself can become round and
mellow with food; a sauce that seems much too rich can change into
something luscious with the right wine. A simple dish and a simple wine,
enjoyed together, are greater than the sum of their parts.

The problem of which wine goes with which food has probably stirred
up more anxiety than anything else in the wine world. There's a myth that a
perfect dish exists for each wine, and that only a master chef or a genius wine
steward can figure out what it is. Is the salmon too assertive for the
Chardonnay? Does the Zinfandel bring out the flavors of the lasagna? What's
the right wine with Velveeta?

As they say in Brooklyn, *fuhgeddabbowdit*. The first revelation: many
good wines taste perfectly fine with a wide variety of foods. In Europe, simple
restaurants keep on hand a generous supply of red and white house wine —
something tasty and cheap, usually from the local region — and serve it with
most meals.

Revelation number two: Just as your reaction to a given wine is
subjective, so is your reaction to a given food and wine combination. In

other words, one person can love a combination and somebody else can hate it, and they'll both be right.

That said, here are some general principles to consider when you choose wine to go with food. Unlike the traditional wine-matching rules (you've heard 'em: red wine with meat, white wine with fish and poultry), these guidelines are more flexible, and depend on both the way the food is prepared and the main ingredient.

The Heartiness Factor

As a first step, think about the *heartiness factor* of the food you're serving. With a little thought, you can classify foods into light-bodied, medium-bodied, and full-bodied or hearty.

The same main ingredient can emerge from the kitchen many different ways; for example, a salad with grilled chicken is probably *light,* a simple roast chicken is medium, and a *coq au vin* braised for hours in red wine with mushrooms, potatoes and salt pork is *hearty.* A plate of scallops sauteed in butter may be *light,* baked salmon is *medium,* and a shellfish soup with tomatoes and garlic is likely to be *hearty.*

Of course, these distinctions depend a lot on your own perceptions and the type of foods you're used to eating. A grilled steak might be thought medium by folks who eat a lot of red meat, hearty by others who don't; if you add creamy, cheesy scalloped potatoes on the side, you've probably tipped the scales in the direction of hearty.

Like foods, wines can also be classified into light-bodied, medium-bodied, and hearty or full-bodied. As you've noticed, some wines are quite subtle and delicate, while others have more pronounced flavors, more tannin, even a "thicker" feel in your mouth. In general, white wines tend to be lighter, red wines heartier.

On the list that follows, some varietals are included in more than one category. That's because it's hard to draw definite lines. Different winemakers and different regions have their own styles that can make a wine lighter or heavier. The characteristics of a certain vintage also make

"For now you understand that bread and wine are twins; that either without the other is but half itself. You are so sensibly aware of this gastronomic truth that, even if you were pinned to the wall, you could not honestly say which is more important on a dinner table blessed with plenty of both."

Angelo M. Pellegrini
in *Lean Years, Happy Years*

their contribution; if the summer was very hot, the wines from that year may be more alcoholic and seem heartier than those from a cooler year. How can you tell? Ask.

Mixing and Matching Flavors

After considering the heartiness factor, take into account the same elements that you consider when you're tasting wine all by itself.

• fruitiness

Fruity wines have a flexibility that lets them harmonize beautifully with the tastes of foods. Perhaps it's the subtly changing quality of the nose (a wine might suggest raspberries, plum and black currants all at once, for example), or perhaps it's the richness that those aromas and flavors add to the wine; in any case, fruitiness is the most important quality of food-friendly wines.

• acidity

Wines higher in acidity are usually most compatible with foods. The acid in the wine can make acidic foods taste mellower, and can contrast well with rich and creamy dishes. The magic works the other way, too: a high-acid food, like a Caesar salad, can bring out the fruitiness in a wine that tastes too acidic on its own.

• sugar

In general, very sweet wines do not bring out the best in foods, any more than cola or fruit punch do. The sugar simply blots out the flavors of the foods. Exceptions are off-dry (slightly sweet) wines with certain foods, and dessert wines with some desserts.

• alcohol

The "hotness" of alcohol can mask the wine's fruity qualities and complicate any match with food. A Riesling at 11 percent alcohol is probably a better candidate to accompany a meal than a Chardonnay at 14 percent.

"Reminds me of my safari in Africa. Somebody forgot the corkscrew and for several days we had to live on nothing but food and water."

W. C. Fields

"Bread and wine of excellent quality are complementary on the dinner table; one strengthens the heart, the other makes it gay. Let us respect them for what each does and strive to have the best of both."

Angelo M. Pellegrini
in *Lean Years, Happy Years*

Light-Bodied Whites

Almost all dry Italian whites	Pinot Blanc
Sauvignon Blanc	Pinot Gris
Chenin Blanc	Gewurztraminer
Riesling	Semillon

Some Chardonnay
those with a lower alcohol level (11-12%), little or no oak aging

Medium-Bodied Whites

Chardonnay
those with a higher alcohol level (13-14%), more oak aging, including many California Chardonnays and white Burgundies such as Puligny-Montrachet, Chassagne-Montrachet, Meursault

Light-Bodied Reds

Gamay (U.S.)	Beaujolais (France)

Bardolino, Valpolicella, Chianti, Dolcetto (Italy)

Medium-Bodied Reds

Pinot Noir	Cabernet Sauvignon
Merlot	Zinfandel
French Burgundy	Côtes du Rhône

Chianti Classico (Italy)

Hearty Reds

Cabernet Sauvignon	Merlot
Zinfandel	Most French Bordeaux

Barolo, Barbaresco, Brunello di Montalcino (Italy)

• tannin

Too much tannin can make wines difficult to match with food because of its bitterness or astringency. Wine buffs sometimes describe overly tannic wines as "stiff," meaning that they lack the graciousness that allows them to join well with foods. Tannic wines can go well with meats, especially grilled meats or other very simple preparations, like roasting.

• oak aging

When wines are aged in oak barrels, especially new oak, they can develop delicious vanilla and toasty flavors. Too much oak, however, can overwhelm the fruitiness of a wine and make it difficult to match with foods.

Next, consider the flavors that a wine suggests in the same way you'd think about pairing flavors in the foods you cook:

•A Pinot Noir with cherry or raspberry notes would complement roast duck with a rich cherry sauce.
•The citrus-like quality of a Sauvignon Blanc might make it a good choice with grilled halibut in a lemon-herb vinaigrette.
•The slight bitterness of a tannic red wine echoes the charred taste of a grilled steak.

Even if you haven't tasted the wine in question, you can make an educated guess about the flavors in certain varietals. Also, labels often have suggestions for matching, so don't forget to read them.

Contrasts between wine and food tastes can work just like the contrasts between different foods in a meal. The same principles you use in cooking apply. For example, hot, spicy flavors often contrast with sweetness in Southwestern cooking or barbecue. So, with Santa Fe-style foods or spicy Cajun shrimp, try a wine with a little residual sugar, like an off-dry Gewurztraminer or Chenin Blanc. Acid (like lemon juice or vinegar) and salt is another pairing frequently seen in cooking: these same complementary flavors make the combination of Champagne, an acidic wine, and salty caviar a classic. (Although it's a classic that's not to everyone's taste. Some feel that caviar makes the Champagne taste metallic and Champagne makes the caviar taste fishy.)

Another successful contrast is between acidic wines, often described as "thin" or "sharp," and the "fat" flavors and feeling in your mouth of oily fish such as salmon, crab and lobster.

Finally, look at the specific foods on the menu:

• the main ingredient

Is it delicate sole or a filet of aged beef? Where are we on the heartiness scale?

• the preparation

Is it grilled, stewed, poached lightly in bouillon, sauteed in butter? What does the cooking method add to the flavors and texture?

• the sauce

Is it based on white wine, butter, rich veal stock or fresh tomatoes? Depending on the dish, sauce can be the most prominent characteristic. An ingredient like chicken or pork tenderloin has a chameleon-like quality, depending on how it's sauced.

Getting the Most from the Experts

Since you aren't going to get a chance to taste every wine before you decide to buy it, the best way to learn about food and wine pairing is to put yourself in the hands of a sharp wine merchant or wine steward.

In a restaurant, tell the waiter what you plan to eat so she can take the menu into account when she helps you choose a wine. And when you go to the wine shop, say exactly what's for dinner: an appetizer of smoked salmon and cream cheese, for example, followed by grilled lamb chops with rosemary and stuffed baked potatoes.

When the merchant recommends a wine or two, ask

why. The response may be something like this: "I'd suggest starting with a fruity Sauvignon Blanc that has enough acid to cut through the fat in the cream cheese and will contrast nicely with the smoked flavor of the salmon. Then I'd go for a Merlot with some tannin to stand up to the lamb chops, but enough fruit to provide a nice contrast with the grilled flavor." If your wine merchant is helpful, every visit will increase your understanding of how to go about pairing wine and food.

"There is a communion of more than our bodies when bread is broken and wine is drunk."

M.F.K. Fisher

Pairing Wines with Herbs and Spices

The best approach is to taste the particular wine you're serving, but these ideas will give you a start.

Wine	Herbs	Spices
Chardonnay	mustard seeds, rosemary, sage, tarragon	clove, ginger, orange zest
Chenin Blanc	anise, chervil, cilantro, dill, fennel, thyme, parsley	allspice, clove, nutmeg
Gewurztraminer	cilantro, mint	black pepper, cardamom, curry, fennel seeds, ginger, nutmeg
Pinot Gris	thyme, savory, chives	coriander, orange zest, star anise, fennel seeds
Riesling	cilantro, coriander seeds, dill, parsley, sage	allspice, black pepper, clove, curry, ginger, mace, nutmeg
Sauvignon Blanc	basil, bay leaf, garlic, oregano, rosemary, savory, thyme	black pepper, cumin, ginger
Semillon	basil, dill, lemon thyme, summer savory	cumin, ginger, sweet paprika
Cabernet Sauvignon	bay leaf, marjoram, parsley, rosemary, thyme	allspice, mace, nutmeg
Merlot	basil, oregano, rosemary, thyme	allspice, mace, nutmeg, star anise
Pinot Noir	mint, rosemary, sage, thyme	allspice, nutmeg, cinnamon, pink peppercorns
Syrah	tarragon, bay leaf, rosemary	mace, clove, juniper, cardamom, white pepper
Zinfandel	tarragon, silver thyme, common thyme, bay leaf, juniper	cinnamon, anise, black pepper, clove

11

Champagne and Sparkling Wine

O ne statistic says a lot about Champagne and sparkling wine in the
United States: ninety percent of it is consumed within three hours of
being purchased, presumably for a celebration. But while the sparkling wine
industry has profited from its association with significant occasions and
erotic interludes, you don't have to relegate bubbly to the occasional toast,
whether it's "Happy new year," or "To us, my little vixen."

First, let's get the terms straight. All Champagne is sparkling wine, but
not all sparkling wine is Champagne. Only sparkling wine made in the
French region of Champagne (east of Paris, and a croissant's throw from
EuroDisney) is Champagne. Everything else, from everywhere else — the rest
of France, Spain, the United States, Australia, wherever — is correctly called
sparkling wine. Don't be fooled by the word Champagne on the label of a
non-French bottle of bubbly; it may be allowed in some places, but it's no
guarantee of quality.

How Bubbly Becomes Bubbly

The seal of approval you should look for instead is the phrase *méthode
champenoise* (Champagne method). It certifies that the bubbles got into the
bottle in the same way that they do in Champagne itself. All wines bubble
during fermentation, but when still (non-sparkling) wines are made, the

bubbles escape into the air and little, if any, effervescence is trapped in the bottle. Champagne, in contrast, goes through a second fermentation in the bottle, which traps the bubbles inside. It's a painstaking and expensive process. Producers who bother to make wine using the *méthode champenoise* usually take great care with other aspects of the winemaking process, too.

Cheap sparkling wine — but never Champagne — goes through the second fermentation in large tanks and is then bottled under pressure. Such wines are labelled *charmat* or *bulk process* in the United States. (This is a quick run-through of the method, just enough to help you read labels as you buy. If you want to know more details, visit one of the many fine sparkling wine makers in the United States, or a Champagne producer in France.)

Decoding the Labels

Sparkling wine has a vocabulary all its own, established by the French. Some of the important words you'll see on labels follow.

• **Brut** identifies the driest sparkling wine. The word can be used on any sparkling wine, no matter where it's from or what grapes are used. It's very common to see brut on a label with one of the other phrases below.

The classic food combination with dry sparkling wine is something salty, like caviar or smoked salmon. It's said that salt in the mouth makes the bubbles more vivacious; one sure thing is that salt makes you thirsty, and thirst makes you drink more bubbly. Brut is your best choice for a before-dinner drink.

• **Blanc de blancs** is made of Chardonnay grapes, which are white; in French, blanc de blancs means a white wine of white grapes. Blanc de blancs is a delicate wine that can be served like brut, with delicate foods.

• **Blanc de noirs** is a white wine made of the dark-colored Pinot Noir grapes (hence *noir* or black), the sort that make red wines like Burgundy. Blanc de noirs is usually a deeper color than blanc de blancs, and often has an attractive pinkish cast, caused by contact with the grape skins. Blanc de noirs is generally fruitier and more robust than blanc de blancs, but the wines will differ depending on the producer.

• **Brut rosé** is a wonderful dry bubbly with a seductive pink color. Perhaps because so many budget rosé wines have been made in the United States, Americans tend to overlook fine sparkling rosés — which are generally a bit more expensive than other sparklers — or think of them as frivolous wines which are beneath consideration.

But a good brut rosé, usually made of Pinot Noir grapes, is fruity and flavorful, and can stand up to substantial foods, like grilled veal chops or roast lamb, with panache. And the color is beautiful, especially by candlelight.

• **Extra-Dry** means slightly sweet. Why such an obviously illogical name developed is lost in the mists of time. It's the best choice to serve with sweet foods — far better than brut, which can taste awfully sour with things like wedding cake or dessert. Try it at brunch or on picnics. In the United States, *spumante* (which is simply Italian for sparkling wine) has also come to mean slightly sweet.

• **Half-Dry (Demi-Sec)** is a sweeter Champagne rarely seen on American shelves. If you come across it, try it with dessert. The Queen Mother kept Veuve Clicquot Half-Dry in her cellar, perhaps for very posh tea parties at Buckingham Palace.

Serving and Storing Sparklers

Experts differ on the origin of the wide, birdbath-style Champagne glass, but everyone agrees that such a glass does absolutely zilch for the wine. The glass's broad area hastens the disappearance of the wonderful bubbles

"In victory we deserve it, in defeat we need it."

Winston Churchill
on Champagne

Be sure Champagne glasses are absolutely clean and free of any soap residue, oil or dampness, or the wine will not bubble.

You'll recognize the rare spoiled bottle of Champagne because it's bitter, flat, and "smells like old socks," as one aficionado puts it. Return it. The very few bad bottles are likely caused by sitting too long on a shelf at the wine shop, or in a refrigerator.

that spent years in the bottle developing, and its shallow bowl allows delicious, crisp Champagne to quickly warm up into a rather nasty, acidic wine. It's also treacherous at a crowded party, because wine can slosh out so easily.

More and more, sparkling wine is served in a *flute* or *tulip* glass. Tall and narrow, it conserves the bubbles as long as possible, and it's easy to hold by the stem, which keeps your hand from warming up the wine. People who think about such things theorize that the bubbles keep forming in the glass because the microscopic roughness of the surface of the glass releases the carbon dioxide trapped in the wine. Since crystal is microscopically rougher than plain glass, more bubbles supposedly form in a crystal glass.

Sparkling wine tastes great with many foods. Its acidity can sweeten acidic flavors like tomato or citrus, and its prickly, bubbly texture makes a nice contrast against smooth or oily foods, like sole or salmon. An increasing number of chefs are treating dry sparkling wine as a kind of upscale beer — like beer, it's yeasty, light, cold and bubbly — and serving it with spicy ethnic cuisines like Chinese, Thai or Latin.

As for serving temperature, straight out of the refrigerator is perfect. Don't use the fridge for long-term storage, though; after a couple of months, the cork will start to lose its elasticity and shrink a bit, so that more of it comes into contact with the wine, and eventually the wine will lose its fruitiness and start to get bitter. Three months is the outside limit. You're better off storing it in the cellar, on its side, until you're definitely ready to drink it.

To Splurge or Not to Splurge

Almost all sparkling wines are aggressively discounted, especially during the holiday season, so shop around. Most people buy French Champagne by name brands, especially famous names like Moët & Chandon, G.H. Mumm, Bollinger, Taittinger, Veuve Clicquot and Louis Roederer. Generally, a bottle of French bubbly will cost around $25, even on special. If you really want to go whole hog, almost all of the famous makers have a top-of-the-line wine that's known in French as the *tête de cuvée* and can cost upwards of $100 a bottle. Probably the most famous *tête de cuvée* is Dom Pérignon, made by Moët & Chandon.

Sometimes wine merchants and big discounters sell lesser known Champagnes at lower prices. Even if you haven't heard of the producer, you're probably pretty safe buying any French Champagne, because the quality standards in France are high.

Outside of France, and in other regions of France, the quality of sparkling wines varies radically. A French connection is no requirement for making delicious bubbly; some American producers are making such good *méthode champenoise* wines in California that French Champagne makers have invested heavily in wineries in Napa and Mendocino. The Spanish and Italians make an array of sparklers, some slightly sweet, some dry, some delicious, some just cheap. Ask your wine merchant to help you find bottles that suit your taste and your wallet.

"I like Champagne because it always tastes as if my foot's asleep."

Art Buchwald

Some people believe the smaller the bubbles the better the Champagne.

Opening Sparkling Wine

1. Remove the foil to expose the wire cage over the cork.

2. The cork is under a lot of pressure, so be careful. Point the bottle away from your loved ones and the Ming vase.

3. Untwist and remove the wire basket with one hand, keeping the other hand over the cork for safety's sake.

4. Tilt the bottle at a 45-degree angle. Grasp the cork in one hand, the bottle in the other.

5. Turn the bottle, not the cork. This way, you're less likely to break off the cork. Rock the cork back and forth gently as you turn the bottle. (It's not as hard as it sounds.)

6. Ease the cork out. If you like, you can hold a napkin or towel in your hand over the cork and use it to slowly ease the cork out.

7. Pour slowly so the wine doesn't foam over the tops of the glasses.

Wildly popping corks is locker-room stuff,
and extremely dangerous besides. Don't do it!

12

Well-Aged Advice
on Old and Young Wines

O n an episode of *The Simpsons,* Homer once treated his nuclear family to a
meal in a snooty restaurant, The Gilded Truffle. ("Homer, look at the
prices!" squeaked Marge. "We could finally get rid of the termites for the cost
of this meal.") When the waiter brought the wine list to the table, Bart
grabbed it, saying, "*I'll* do the honors."

A pained expression came over Bart's little face as he scanned the list.
"No, no, no, *no,*" he groaned. "My God! What passes for a wine list these
days!"

With a gesture of disgust, Bart put down the list. "Just bring us a bottle
of your *freshest* wine," he commanded.

Well, Bart Simpson is rarely cited as a wine expert, but the lad's
instinct wasn't bad: young wines usually are a good bet. Although that TV
commercial with Orson Welles intoning, "We sell no wine before its time,"
implied otherwise, the vast majority of the world's wines are ready to drink as
soon as they're put in the bottle, usually within a year of harvest. They may
change a bit over time, but they probably won't improve significantly, and in
just a few years their flavors will fade.

It Was a Very Good Year

You'll see a year written on many wine labels. That year is called the
vintage. In the United States, by law, 95 percent of the wine in that bottle had

to be made from grapes harvested in that year. (Other countries have similar laws.)

You'll hear wine enthusiasts talk about "good years," "bad years" and even "great years." Since most winemakers are farmers, they, like all farmers, are greatly affected by the weather. Whether a frost kills tender young buds, how much rain falls, whether the sun shines enough while the grapes are ripening — all are factors that contribute to the quality of a vintage. In places where sunny weather is virtually guaranteed, like parts of California, the differences between vintages can be small; in more northerly regions where the weather is more variable, like Germany or northern France, differences between vintages can be somewhat more significant. Modern winemaking technology has also found ways to soften some of the effects of bad weather.

As you become familiar with the wines from various countries and regions, you may eventually notice differences between vintages. Some are slight, others more pronounced. Differences in vintage quality can account for something you may notice in the wine shop: two similar wines from the same region or the same winery at quite different prices. The lower-priced wine could be the product of a lesser vintage. But wine can also be priced lower when a sunny year produces a bumper crop of grapes, leaving the wineries with more wine to sell. Your wine merchant can sometimes explain such price differences.

Consumers often believe that a wine with the vintage marked on the label is somehow a better wine than a *non-vintage* or *NV* wine, which is a wine that blends the products of two harvests or more. However, that's not necessarily the case. Many wineries offer excellent wines that blend grapes from several vintages, and some are less expensive than single-vintage wines. If you buy only wines with a vintage on the label, you may miss some delicious bottlings. Winemakers have many reasons for making non-vintage wines; commonly, they want to balance out the qualities of several years of harvests. Read the label when you see a wine bottle without a vintage. You may get some information that will make you want to try the wine.

Worrying about vintage years should be a fairly small consideration. The big exception is when you're buying wines to age. As you'll see in the next section, that's when vintage is more important.

When Older Can Mean Better — and Why

Only a small percentage of wines improve with age. Red wines from the Bordeaux region of France are responsible for much of the mystique of old wine. Their very names — including Chateau Lafite-Rothschild, Chateau Latour and Chateau Margaux — have become synonymous with wealth, class and English guys in tweed coats sitting in leather armchairs and puffing on cigars. The great reds of Burgundy, too, add to the aura, especially Domaine de la Romanée-Conti, whose 1990 vintage became the world's most expensive newly released wine ever in 1993, at almost $900 a bottle.

Many factors combine to make a wine that will last and improve over years or decades. As a general rule, only red wines improve with age, because they contain more tannin than white wines, and tannin is a major component that gives wines the staying power that lets them age. Certain acids also contribute to a wine's aging ability.

Only a few white wines improve with age. Most go downhill pretty fast after three years or so. Some whites from Burgundy, Germany and the Loire Valley of France age well, due largely to their high acidity, which keeps them fresh.

Tannin alone doesn't determine whether a wine will get better over time. If you could take just any wine with a lot of tannin in it, throw it in the cellar for ten years or so and have something spectacular emerge, there'd be nothing special about old wine. Instead, the legendary aged wines result from a combination of the qualities of certain grapes, the marriage of the grape variety to the place where it is grown, the craft of winemaking and the whims of Mother Nature.

Only a very few of the thousands of varieties of grapes can be made into wine that improves over time.

Chief among them are Cabernet Sauvignon and Merlot, which are used in Bordeaux, and Pinot Noir, which makes the red wines of Burgundy. When young, some Cabernet Sauvignon can be very stiff and puckery, even unpleasant. (Think back to the taste and sensation of too much tannin in the tea-tasting exercise.) But the tannin helps the wine age. Eventually, if the wine had just the right balance of fruitiness, tannin and other elements to start with, it will develop wonderful, complex flavors in twenty (or thirty or forty) years.

French red Burgundy, made from Pinot Noir, can run the gamut from fruity wines that are delightful to drink young, to stiff and unapproachable young wines that come into their own over years in the cellar. Among other red wines that can age well are Zinfandel and such Italian wines as Barolo, made with the Nebbiolo grape.

The winemaker makes a number of decisions about blending, fermentation, barrel-aging and other factors that contribute to whether a wine is best when it is young or old. Incidentally, the two aren't mutually exclusive; a wine that is a pleasure to drink young can also age and change, and whether it's more delicious sooner or later is often a matter of individual preference. Most important, as wine critic Robert M. Parker Jr. writes, "Balance is everything in wine, and wines that taste too tart or tannic [when young] rarely ever age into flavorful, distinctive, charming beverages."

Finally, there's the question of vintage: the characteristics of the grapes during a given year, which are largely determined by the weather. While differences between vintages may be less significant for younger wines, they frequently take on greater importance as wines age. In many books about wine, you'll find vintage charts that rank the quality of wine made in various regions in various years. They can be useful if you're in the market for older wines, or buying young wines for your cellar in hopes that they'll age well.

Perhaps the longest-lived wines of all are dessert wines, especially the Sauternes of the Bordeaux region, of which Chateau d'Yquem is the most celebrated. The sugar and gluconic acid in those wines serve a preservative function. At a tasting of d'Yquem in 1993, the top three vintages were the 1847, 1874 and 1929. (Those dates are not typographical errors!)

What's So Great About Old Wine?

The differences between old and young wines are usually obvious to the eye. Young white wines are generally light straw or gold colors; older whites turn deep gold, amber, even brown, like sherry. Young red wines tend to be very intense in color with bright ruby, garnet and purple shades. Older reds, on the other hand, can be brick and brownish; they can lose color and look almost clear around the edges when you tilt a glass of wine and hold it up to light.

Young wines tend to be fruitier than old ones, and to taste more of grapes. A fine older wine will have some fruitiness remaining, but its flavors and aromas will be more complex and subtle than those of young wines, possibly suggesting cedar, earth, chocolate, truffles or leather.

Wine experts disagree, sometimes heatedly, over whether old or young wines are more rewarding to drink. There's little question that some wines reach the height of their perfection only after several years in the cellar. Drinking a perfectly aged old Bordeaux or Burgundy can be sublime. On the other hand, you can also enjoy wine all your life without ever uncorking an old bottle. Plenty of folks prefer fruity, lively young wines; some even insist that drinking old wine is not pleasant at all, and that the people who claim they enjoy it are the sort of hopeless snobs who'd applaud the emperor's new clothes.

For Those Who Drink Young

• **White wines** generally shouldn't be any more than two or three years old, or they'll lose their fresh, fruity qualities.

• **Sparkling wines** and non-vintage Champagnes are generally ready to drink when they're bottled, so there's no advantage to aging them. They don't age in the bottle and they're not ever going to get any better than they are right this minute, so don't put that gift bottle of

Don't put wine in the refrigerator until a day or two, at most, before you serve it.

Champagne in the refrigerator for two years. Drink it and enjoy it.

Vintage-dated Champagnes are an exception to the drink-it-now rule. If stored carefully, they will age in the bottle for up to ten years, developing delicious nutty flavors.

• **Many red wines** are easy to drink young. In the United States, look for Pinot Noir, Gamay and varieties from the Rhône region of southern France, like Syrah and Grenache. Merlot has become popular among Americans because it has a full-bodied flavor but can taste better young than Cabernet. Other good bets are French Beaujolais (a lighter red that's meant to be drunk within a year or two at most) and Italian Dolcetto.

As for Cabernet Sauvignon, a growing trend in the United States is to make it specifically to drink young, in a softer, less tannic style than traditional French Bordeaux. It also can be blended with kinder and gentler varietals, most commonly Merlot, that take the tannic edge off. If you see a Cabernet that's less than five or six years old on a wine list in your price range, ask for a description of it. The wine steward may assure you that it's "soft" or "approachable," or that it's "drinking well," or he may ever-so-tactfully steer you to another part of the wine list.

Storing Wine for the Long Term

For a couple of months or so, you can keep wine without damage almost anywhere that's not very warm or in direct sunlight. But if you've got a few bottles you'd like to age, keep them lying on their side in a dark place where the temperature stays constant between 55 and 65 degrees. A corner of the basement is often ideal, as long as it's not near a heating vent.

Shopping for Wine

I f you're serious about expanding your wine horizons, the single most valuable thing you can do is get to know your local wine merchant. A good wine merchant can be an unsurpassed resource for information, recommendations and creative ideas.

First, though, you have to separate the good from the bad. Take a look around at a shop selling wine. Does it specialize in wine, or is wine just an afterthought in an ordinary liquor store? Is there an intriguing selection of wines from different countries, different regions? What about storage: are wine bottles lying down in a cool, dark place, or are they roasting in a sunny window, or stacked next to the heating vent?

If the shop passes a visual inspection, the next step is testing the staff. Unless you're trying to stock your cellar in the chaos of New Year's Eve, salespeople should be happy to help you and listen to your needs. Ask about a couple of the wines that interest you. You should be able to get a clear, understandable description of the wine. (If you can't follow the description, it's not your problem; it's the problem of the person who's doing the describing.) The classic test is to tell the salesperson what you're planning to have for dinner, and ask for a recommendation. The more specific you are, the better this test works. Instead of saying, "We're having pasta," you'll learn more about the wine — and the shop — by saying "We're having pasta with a wild mushroom cream sauce," or "We're having pasta with tomato sauce, black olives and spicy Italian sausage." A well-informed clerk should give you several suggestions, and tell you why each wine would work with the food you're serving. You can also ask for something like "a simple white wine to serve for a cocktail party in our backyard," or "a tawny port that's not too expensive."

"The Best $5 Wine I've Got"

Never be afraid to talk about price. If you don't believe me, listen to Portland, Oregon, wine merchant Matthew Elsen. "There's nothing dishonorable about asking for a good $5 bottle of wine," he says. "I live on a budget myself. If a customer wants to spend $5, I'll give her the best $5 bottle of wine I've got." If you encounter a condescending attitude, if your price guidelines aren't respected, or if your questions aren't answered clearly and willingly, go elsewhere.

Savvy wine merchants want to do more than sell you a bottle of wine; they want to make you a regular customer. "There's no such thing as a stupid question," Elsen adds. "I love the person who comes in and asks for a recommendation, and I'm very selective about what I suggest. It becomes a great point of personal honor not to sell schlock. I want him to come back." Elsen finds it an irresistible challenge when a customer says, "I had a bottle of Famous Name Winery Cabernet Sauvignon for $30, and I'd like you to give me something that tastes just as good for $10."

If a bottle is spoiled, the shop should take it back, pleasantly, and offer you a replacement or a refund. You can't tell simply by looking at a bottle if the wine inside is in good condition, but three conditions may indicate that a bottle of wine has been badly stored or subjected to damaging heat:

- A cork that has pushed a little ways out of the bottle.

- Wine that has seeped out (the bottle may be sticky).

If you can't get help at the supermarket, keep a lookout for workers stocking the wine shelves. Often these people don't work for the supermarket — they work for wholesalers, and are sometimes very knowledgeable about wine in general, or at least about the various labels they sell.

- A larger-than-usual air space between the bottom of the cork and the top of the liquid in the bottle. (The technical name for that space is *ullage,* pronounced YOU-ledge.) It shouldn't be much more than a half-inch. If in doubt, compare the bottle to some of the others around.

If a wine you've tasted or read about isn't in stock, a good wine merchant should be willing to order it for you. Don't expect a wine merchant to give free tastings of several wines, however, like wineries often do. The merchant has to buy the wine, and few small businesses can afford to give away much of what they're supposed to sell.

Reading the Ratings

Several respected and influential wine authorities critically review wines and rate them on a numerical scale. Best known are Robert M. Parker Jr., the author of many fine books on wine and publisher of the *Wine Advocate* newsletter, and the editors of the *Wine Spectator,* a magazine covering the wine world. *Wine Spectator* ratings are based on the averaged opinions of a committee of tasters, while Parker's ratings are based on Parker's taste alone. Both Parker and *Wine Spectator* rankings use a 100-point scale. (Some magazines, especially British and European ones, rate wines on a 20-point scale.)

A good rating can have a tremendous effect on sales of a given wine, and sometimes on everything else made by the same winemaker. A low score, on the other hand, can stop a wine — or even a winery — dead in its tracks, commercially speaking.

Ratings can be an extremely helpful guide to buying wine; I use them frequently myself. The descriptions themselves are, for me, often more enlightening than the numerical ratings, because they give me a sense of the wine's character before making a buying decision. The rankings can also be a guide through unfamiliar territory if you're interested in trying a type of wine that you don't know much about.

In big shops that sell wine quickly, there's nothing wrong with bottles that stand up on the shelves instead of lying on their sides

On ratings: "Anybody can taste the difference between a 70 and a 90, but only God knows the difference between an 86 and an 87."

Bill Hatcher,
Domaine Drouhin Oregon

Don't take the recommendations to extremes. Even the *Wine Spectator* chastised readers for getting hung up only on the highest numbers, and rejecting wines that rank under 90. Editor Harvey Steiman wrote, "I feel sorry for these misguided souls. They are missing out on so many lovely wines that rate in the 80s . . . We think these are fine wines that deserve a place on any dining table." In fact, most of the wines ranked in the 80s are the ones you want to drink now, and many of the 90s are given extra points primarily because of their aging potential.

In many wine shops, you'll see reprints of a ranking and a paragraph-length review from Parker or the *Wine Spectator* hanging beneath some of the bottles. (Sometimes you'll see them from other magazines too, like *Decanter,* a British magazine, or *Wine and Spirits*.) Used intelligently, these shelf-talkers can be a great aid to choosing wine, especially if you're shopping at a discount store or supermarket that doesn't otherwise offer much help to wine buyers.

A fun tasting project for a group of friends is to pick up a copy of the Wine Spectator *at your local newsstand or wine shop and buy several wines that it rates in the "Buying Guide" section. Taste them blind, score them on a 100-point scale and perhaps jot down a few descriptive phrases. Compare your group's rankings and descriptions to those of the magazine's reviewers. You'll usually find plenty of room for discussion.*

Big Bottles, Little Bottles

Good wines come in several different packages. Here are the most common sizes you'll see:

• Most fine table wine comes in a *750 milliliter* (ml) bottle; that's what wine people usually mean when they talk about a *bottle.* It is a little less than a quart, and contains five to six glasses of wine.

• Half that size is, obviously, *375 ml*, also known as a *split* or *half-bottle.* Sweet dessert wines, which are served in very small amounts, are usually bottled in 375s.

• A new size catching on slowly in the United States is *500 ml*. Despite resistance from wholesalers, who find carrying another bottle size a nuisance, restaurants are starting to put this ideal "wine for two" size on wine lists.

• Then there's the *187 ml* bottle, the wine world's answer to the beer can. You could call it "wine for one," and it's great in a picnic cooler. It's used mainly for low-priced wines, and several makers of sparkling wine are using it too.

• Some fine red wines are bottled in *magnums,* which contain 1.5 liters (twice the size of the 750), or even *double magnums.* Supposedly the larger size makes wines age better. Sometimes you'll encounter a magnum on a restaurant wine list; it can be a good deal if you're serving a group of eight or ten.

• Other than the occasional magnum, you'll rarely see fine wines in bottles larger than 750 ml. Bigger bottles, whether they're labeled with a varietal name or not, are usually "jug" quality wine. They can be pleasant, though, and are certainly economical if the gang is coming over for spaghetti.

Few things delight me more than finding myself in a restaurant with a good selection of half-bottles on the wine list. My husband and I love wine, but especially when we're out to dinner and going to be driving afterward, the last thing we want to do is overindulge. When half-bottles are available, we can order two different wines and enjoy them both without spending a bundle. (Sometimes half-bottles are listed in a separate section on the wine list, so be sure to check, or ask the waiter.)

"The difference in a trial of wine by the consumer and the expert is that the former seeks for something agreeable, something to praise, while the latter seeks for a fault, a blemish or something to condemn."

Arpad Haraszthy

Favorite Food and Wine Combinations

Ripe brie cheese, green grapes, and Chenin Blanc.

Rich, juicy dark meat of roast duck and a French Burgundy.
(Jim Smith, Wine Club, San Francisco)

Cold cracked Dungeness crab, homemade
lemon mayonnaise, fresh French bread, and a crisp, fruity Sauvignon Blanc.

Grilled flour tortillas and spicy salsa,
with a red wine so full-bodied you can practically chew it.
(John Sedlar, chef, Bikini, Santa Monica, Calif.)

A rare hamburger, topped with a thick slice
of grilled onion and crumbled Stilton cheese, and a glass of Merlot.

Chicken in a mushroom cream sauce,
and a Chardonnay with hints of vanilla and lemon.

Broiled tiny lamb chops, browned potatoes and perfectly fresh green beans with an
elegant, well-aged bottle of first-growth Bordeaux, rich, fruity and a little tannic.
(Sara Matthews, photographer, N.Y.)

Spicy-sweet barbecued ribs with Zinfandel.

Eggs Benedict and Pinot Gris.

A spicy chicken and andouille gumbo with
an equally spicy Gewurztraminer, either dry or off-dry.
(Gene Bourg, restaurant reviewer, *New Orleans Times-Picayune*)

Fettuccine al pesto with an Italian Pinot Grigio.

Ordering Wine in Restaurants

T he wine list crashes down on the table, looking as thick as the latest thousand-page Michener novel — if Michener novels had padded maroon imitation-alligator covers and gold-embossed curlicues. Believe me, only the biggest wine fanatics don't experience a little shudder of fear when they come face-to-face with such a thing. Normal people are terrified of getting lost in a nightmarish landscape where Burgundian villagers toil in obscure vineyards of the Friuli along the banks of the Rhine, and all the bottles cost at least $80.

Take heart: a long list is often a sign that you're in a place where people care about wine, and where there's likely to be someone knowledgeable who can help you out.

Help! I Need Somebody! (Not Just Anybody)
The first order of business is to determine who can help you. The person in charge of the wine at a restaurant can go by several titles. Only a few restaurants have someone specifically concerned with wine, who is generally called the *wine steward.* In French, that's *sommelier* (saw-mel-YAY), a term which is also used in the United States. I've also been in some restaurants where the wine guy (or gal) is called the *cellarmaster.*

Many wine stewards today believe that fancy titles and terribly formal etiquette get in the way of enjoying wine. There seems to be less and less *attitude* among people selling wine. The terrifying guy in a tuxedo called Pierre or Gustav who always speaks in whispers is, thank heaven, going the way of the dodo bird, even in expensive restaurants. In the United States, restaurants are increasingly training all the waiters to sell wine.

A wine steward or waiter is there to give you information and help you get a wine that will really add to your meal. I see a funny reverse psychology at work in restaurants all the time. It seems that the more people know about wine, the more questions they ask the wine steward, while customers who are relative novices often order the first familiar thing they see, or just slam the wine list shut in a panic. In short, the people who could learn the most are often too intimidated to try. Ask a few questions next time you're ordering wine, and you're likely to be pleasantly surprised by a friendly, helpful response.

How to Read a Wine List

When the wine list arrives at the table, your first step should be to browse through the entire list to see how it's organized. Most wine lists are grouped into broad categories (usually red wines, white wines, sparkling wines and dessert wines), and then into varietals (such as Cabernet Sauvignon and Merlot) or regions of the world (such as California, Australia, Chianti or Burgundy).

Once you and your companions have decided what you're going to eat, call the wine steward over to the table. Tell him what you're planning to order, and perhaps give him a sense of what you'd like to drink: "We like wines that aren't too acidic," or "I had a Sauvignon Blanc last week that I really enjoyed. Do you think something like that would go with the foods we've chosen?"

A bottle of wine contains five to six glasses. If there are more than four or five guests and they've ordered a wide variety of foods, you might want to order two bottles — a white and a red — simultaneously, so everyone can have a choice.

Never accept a bottle of wine that is not opened at your table.

The more you make it clear that you are interested in wine and have some opinions and preferences, the more attention you're likely to get from the staff. Here's a situation where, no matter how much experience you have, you can easily do exactly what the wine experts do. *I can't emphasize this enough: ask, ask, ask!*

Making Yourself Clear

At this point, a good wine steward or waiter may ask a few more questions about wines you prefer or wines you've enjoyed in the past. Don't worry. This is not an insidious wine snob's method of exposing your ignorance. Look at the waiter as a conscientious salesperson who is trying to help you buy something you'll like. Especially in a restaurant specializing in a particular ethnic or regional cuisine, don't retreat to the old standbys. If well-informed help is available, be adventurous.

Even if you're not asked, don't hesitate to say how much you want to spend — "We want something around $20," or "Let's keep it under $30." After talking it over, ask the wine steward to recommend and describe two or three

---

Two Great Questions to Ask in a Restaurant

Evan Goldstein, director of the Sterling Vineyards School of Service and Hospitality in the Napa Valley, contributed his two favorite queries. "I guarantee these will endear you to wine-knowledgeable waiters," he said.

- What is the best value on this list?

"Waiters are always delighted to share their pet favorites."

- Do you have any wines that are not on the list?

"Sometimes restaurants have a few things put away in the back that are not on any list. Maybe they only have a few bottles of a wine that's much in demand, which they parcel out to people who are smart enough to ask."

possibilities in roughly your price range. Note that the wine steward has an interest in getting you to spend more if possible, because if you order something more expensive he makes more money (on tips, and because many wine stewards receive a commission on wine sold). But he also has an interest in keeping you satisfied.

Pay attention if a wine steward you trust recommends something truly special that's a few dollars more; given the cost of dining out, it's silly to miss a wonderful experience for the equivalent of a dollar or so a glass. You'll soon feel comfortable making these decisions, especially at a restaurant that you visit fairly often.

A few restaurants that are very serious about wine have both a regular wine list and a *reserve list* of older and more expensive wines. Generally, you have to request the reserve list. If it's a special occasion, you're familiar with the restaurant, and you feel like splurging, ask to see it. You can also ask to see it if you're simply interested in browsing; there's no obligation to choose a wine from it. You'll usually see prices ranging from $50 to well into the hundreds.

A welcome new trend is the short list of wines carefully selected to complement the chef's style. You're probably better off with twenty excellent wines to choose from, in a price range appropriate for the restaurant, than you would be trying to pick through 150 wines that run the gamut from vintage to vinegar.

The Contingency Plan

Things don't always go smoothly. Maybe you've got a waiter who has no talent for talking about wine, or who just won't take the time to find out what you want and make intelligent recommendations. Maybe you suspect that he's hiding his ignorance behind a few catch-phrases, like "full-bodied" or "smooth." In a Spanish restaurant, I once asked the waiter to help me choose among the 15 different Rioja wines (a Spanish red) on the wine list. "They're all dry!" she chirped.

What can you do? Try asking to speak to the manager or whoever buys wine for the restaurant. You may stumble on someone who knows what they're doing. Sometimes, if I'm not getting any useful information from the waiter, I'll cut to the chase and ask, "Is there anyone more familiar with the wine list whom I could talk to?"

Susan Sokol Blosser, CEO of Sokol Blosser Winery in Oregon, has a practical strategy. "When the staff doesn't know what's going on, I'll sometimes ask, 'What's your best-selling wine?' or 'What have you served that people seem to like?'" she says. "At least that way I get something drinkable."

Another useful approach is to hone in on a category of wine that you're familiar with, like American Chardonnay, say, or Merlot. Or, if you've become familiar with several favorite wineries, stick to their wines when in doubt. A warning sign: if the wine list doesn't specify producers and vintage years, you're probably in a place that doesn't take pride in its wine cellar. That could translate into spotty quality. Order something you know well.

A difficult situation arises when you order a wine that's been recommended and you don't like it, or it's not as the waiter described it. If the wine isn't actually spoiled, what happens next really comes down to the restaurant's policy on customer service. I usually speak up, politely, and explain why the wine doesn't live up to my expectations. In several cases, restaurants have been willing to replace the wine with something different, and only charge for one bottle.

> *Don't order wine without knowing how much it costs. You don't want to discover, as one friend of mine did, that the half-bottle of Bordeaux he ordered on the waiter's verbal recommendation cost $65. I love surprises — but not this kind.*

The Serving Ceremony,
or Some Clever Things to Do with That Cork

The pomp and circumstance of being served wine in restaurants can seem as strange as something out of the court of Queen Victoria. But the whole drill is really pretty simple, as long as you know what to expect.

• The waiter shows you the bottle. Don't just nod: look at the label, and make sure it's the same wine, and the same vintage, that you ordered. I've found that waiters accidentally bring the wrong bottles surprisingly often. They also may substitute vintages without mentioning it — which could mean paying a lot more money, or getting a wine that's over the hill. So double-check that the wine you've got is the wine you asked for.

• The waiter opens the bottle and puts the cork on the table. This tradition may have developed as a way of guaranteeing that the wine you've ordered is actually what's in the bottle, and that an unscrupulous restaurateur hasn't surreptitiously filled your bottle of Chateau Big Bucks with some junk. Most corks have the name of the winery written on them, so you could read the cork and make sure it matches the label.

Examining the cork might give you a clue or two to the probable condition of the wine, though experts disagree on how much you can actually tell. Anyway, you'll be tasting the wine itself momentarily, which will tell you a lot more than the cork will.

But hey, you can play along. Pick up the cork and roll it between your fingers. If it's from a red wine, one end should be stained red. Any cork should be somewhat moist and flexible. If it's brittle or crumbly, that may mean that the wine has been stored upright for a long time, or that it was stored somewhere with very low humidity. That could mean that the wine is spoiled, but not necessarily.

Some people like to smell the cork. I say don't bother: A cork that's just been pulled out of a bottle smells mostly like, well, *cork*. Another perfectly acceptable option is to ignore the cork completely. For a giggle, you can put it in the ashtray.

• The waiter will pour a small amount of wine into your glass. You are now expected to say whether the wine is "good," that is, *not spoiled*. You don't have to give it a rating from 1 to 100, or describe the vineyard that it was grown in, or talk about your deep personal friendship with the winemaker, or make any profound comments at all.

Take your time. Use your eyes, nose and mouth. Look at the wine and make sure it's clear, not cloudy, and that nothing (like, for example, pieces of that damn cork) is floating in it. Swirl it energetically in your glass and inhale, seeking out the pleasant, fresh aromas of a wine in

Some restaurants serve a plain-wrap "house" wine, which is usually described by color — red, white or rosé. It typically comes in unlabeled carafes, and it's inexpensive, which is usually about the best thing that can be said for it. If you're looking for something cheap and cheerful with a simple meal, it may do the trick, but don't expect anything very special. Before ordering, at least ask what winery it comes from; you're entitled to know what you're spending your money on.

good condition. Finally, taste and swish it around your mouth a bit, to double-check the impressions your nose gave you.

• Nod to the waiter, or say something like "That's fine," or "Very good," or "Thank you." ("Wow, best stuff I ever tasted," is acceptable if you're so moved.) The waiter will then fill the glasses of everyone at the table, filling yours last.

The Wine Steward's Secrets: Getting the Best Values

If you think wine costs too much in restaurants, you're not alone. No less an authority than *New York Times* wine columnist Frank Prial has lamented that high restaurant wine prices are making patrons decide, "Wine is a luxury they can do without."

The standard mark-up on most wine lists is two-and-a-half to three times the wholesale cost of the bottle. Thus, a wine that wholesales for $10 (and sells for about $15 retail) can set you back $25 or more in a restaurant. Restaurant owners will tell you that it is expensive to serve wine and maintain a well-stocked cellar. Granted. But as consumers become more cost-conscious, I think that restaurants are shooting themselves in the foot by insisting on profit margins that make ordering a bottle of wine as expensive as inviting one more guest to dinner.

If you're looking for the best value on a wine list, experts suggest you concentrate on wines priced between $25 and $35. You'll find your best combination of quality and price are often in this price range, around the middle of the list, rather than at the bottom.

Here's why: A bottle listed for $18 to $20 is probably marked up three or even four times from its wholesale price. Many restaurants don't even include wines for under $20 or so on their lists, so they mark up everything to at least that level. They look at cheaper wines as an opportunity to take larger profits. However, as you get above $25, you'll find higher-quality wines that are multiplied fewer times. If they were marked up as many times as the cheaper wines they'd quickly become unaffordable. A wine that costs $30 in a restaurant might retail for $12 (a mark-up of 2.5 times) while a $20 wine might retail for only $5 (a mark-up of four times). The more-expensive wine actually represents the better — less inflated — value.

Exercising Your Options

Look for restaurants that have a commitment to reasonably priced wines. More and more establishments are offering some bottles for around $20, plenty of choices at $25 to $30, and moderately priced wines by the glass. Patronize them, order wine, and tell the management how pleased you are to have a choice of less-expensive wines.

When you find yourself in a restaurant with few reasonably priced selections, voice your opinion, not by grumbling under your breath, but by politely asking to see the owner, manager or wine buyer. Explain that you'd like to see more choices in the lower price ranges. Don't be embarrassed — wine professionals are just as likely to make this observation as anyone else. Only a snob thinks that all wines are expensive, and real wine lovers know there are treasures at any price. The bonus to this strategy is that the manager's reaction will give you an idea about whether you want to patronize the restaurant in the future.

More and more smart restaurateurs are approaching wine sales with an eye to taking less profit per bottle but selling more wine overall. Some restaurants are selling wines at wine-shop retail prices. Not long ago, a restaurant in Manhattan's theater district was using its wine list as an enticement to get diners in the door, selling wines at certain hours for just $1 over its wholesale cost — less than retail. Even the fabled Four Seasons restaurant in New York started what, for it, is a bargain list, of thirty wines for $30 or less.

Wine by the Glass

Once upon a time, if you wanted just a glass of wine rather than a whole bottle, you'd order a generic "white" or "red" and something — heaven knows what, and nobody asked anyway — would show up. That's still true in a lot of places.

In better restaurants, however, selling premium wines by the glass became a trend when technology provided an answer to the problem of keeping open bottles of costly wine fresh: the Cruvinet and similar machines that replace the air in open bottles with nitrogen. Lately, more and more restaurants take pride in offering several fine wines by the glass, frequently selecting them with certain dishes on the menu or the chef's style of cooking in mind.

By-the-glass selections may give you a good opportunity to experiment, especially if you find yourself in a restaurant where the cooking doesn't lend itself to an obvious wine choice. The sophisticated Creole dishes at Emeril's in New Orleans and the complex Pacific Rim curries at Wild Ginger in Seattle both come to mind, and both restaurants sell carefully chosen wines by the glass.

Wine by the glass is an especially good value if you're eating by yourself or with only one other person, because it gives you the opportunity to try several wines without springing for whole bottles that you probably won't finish. The wines are frequently chosen from wineries' and distributors' monthly specials, so they may be well priced. The down side is that restaurateurs sometimes dump stuff that is not moving well or is over the hill into their by-the-glass offerings.

How can you tell the class from the dross? Follow the same rules that apply for ordering wine by the bottle. Insist on speaking to someone knowledgeable. State your own preferences, say what food you've ordered and ask for

In some states, you can take a partially finished bottle of wine home from a restaurant. Check on the law where you live. The restaurant will typically cork the bottle and put it in a bag for you. (State law may require that you put an opened bottle in the trunk of your car rather than in the passenger compartment; check on that one, too, to avoid embarrassing conversations with the highway patrol.)

I've sometimes had to argue with reluctant or ill-informed restaurateurs on this one, because few customers take advantage of this opportunity. But why buy good wine and leave it behind?

a recommendation. One advantage over ordering full bottles: you can ask for a taste of the wine you're considering and the restaurant will often oblige at no charge.

Ordering by the glass may not be the most economical approach when you're with a larger group, but it has its advantages — everyone can have exactly what they want, to go with exactly what they've ordered.

One vexing problem with ordering wine by the glass is that it sometimes comes at the wrong temperature and there's not much you can do about it. Obviously, if it's too cool you can wait for it to warm up a bit. But if it's too warm, you can't put a wine glass in an ice bucket, and plopping in some ice cubes isn't a very good idea. If the problem's serious enough to interfere with enjoying the wine, explain to the waiter, and send it back.

When you've ordered a bottle of wine, don't let the waiter push you by filling the glasses too fast. Emptying the bottle at high speed is a common ploy to get you to order more. Especially when you're drinking white wine, which is probably being kept cold in an ice bucket, the last thing you want to do is let it warm up while sitting in your glass. Ask the waiter to slow down.

Bringing Your Own Wine to a Restaurant

Under some circumstances, you can bring your own wine to a restaurant. The first thing to do is call the restaurant and ask if you may do so. They will probably quote you a *corkage* charge, which can vary from $5 to $20, depending on how posh the place is. Charges up to $10 are fairly common, but they can be higher at more expensive restaurants.

These fees are supposed to cover the restaurant's costs of serving the wine and providing glassware. This, of course, is ridiculous. If you were drinking water, the waiter would put glasses on the table and refill them without a fee. While it's true that serving wine can sometimes be more time-consuming than serving water, corkage is really designed to compensate somewhat for the income the restaurant is losing by not selling you wine.

It's almost never a good idea to bring your own wine on your first visit to a well-regarded restaurant. Looking over the wine list is part of getting to know a place; many of the bottles listed at restaurants with good chefs and wine buyers are chosen to complement the style of food served. You'd be making a mistake to miss this opportunity to learn about new wines and food and wine combinations. However, once you've been to a place and seen the strengths and weaknesses of its wine list, you could consider bringing your own.

Bring your own wine only when it's unlikely to be found on a restaurant's list. The trick is to look like you've got a special bottle to drink, not that you're trying to save your pennies. It's considered tacky to drag along a bottle of something that you can find in any wine shop.

Instead, use a little originality. Good candidates are: anything you've kept in your cellar for a few years that isn't in the stores anymore (extra points for very old wines); wines that are relatively expensive ($30 and up) in shops, like high-end French and Italian wines (these could cost way over $50 in a restaurant, and most establishments probably don't have a large selection of them); something you bought at that obscure little winery in Rhode Island or in the Okanagan Valley of British Columbia, or a late-harvest dessert wine, found on few wine lists.

When you arrive, hand the bottle over to the maitre d', perhaps with some low-key instructions like, "I think this could be chilled a bit, thanks," or "We'd like to drink this with our main course, please."

The wine should be served with the same tasting ceremony as a bottle you've ordered off the list. This isn't as silly as it seems. Obviously, you're not going to send the wine back. But if it happens to be spoiled, you'll want to know that before the server fills everyone's glass. And you'll want to have a chance to order something else off the wine list.

When it comes to tipping, don't just figure 15 percent of the corkage charge; if the service was good, add a little extra to reflect what a purchased bottle of wine would have added to your bill.

At the Olde Port Inn, in Avila Beach, California (near San Luis Obispo), owner Leonard Cohen is a real wine buff. Many of the wines on his list are priced at wine-shop retail or less. And the only corkage fee he asks for is a taste of the wine the patrons have brought in.

A much-appreciated courtesy is to offer a taste of a special bottle to your server. But don't think that it replaces a tip — it doesn't.

Favorite Food and Wine Combinations

Grilled swordfish with a tomato-and-onion salsa and a crisp Italian Pinot Grigio.
(Matthew Elsen, wine merchant, Portland, Ore.)

Sushi rolls of incredibly fresh raw tuna,
pickled cucumber and sticky Japanese rice with a Semillon-Chardonnay blend.

Bittersweet chocolate brownies and Beaujolais,
especially the grand cru called St.-Amour.

Grilled veal chop, with the fat crisp and
caramelized, roasted potatoes, and a brut rosé sparkling wine.
(John Scharffenberger, Scharffenberger Cellars, Anderson Valley, Calif.)

Caesar salad and a citrusy, acidic Sauvignon Blanc.

Roasted herb-encrusted rack of lamb or venison, or any big pungent juicy hunk of
meat, with a massive bottle of the heaviest Italian red you can find, especially Barolo.
(Jeff Prather, Ray's Boathouse, Seattle)

Apricot or peach tart with a late-harvest Muscat or Gewurztraminer.

Lamb shanks braised until they're falling-off-the-bone tender,
with white beans and a Cabernet Sauvignon, or a good Barolo.

Almond biscotti dipped into a nice late-harvest Riesling,
just until the edges are soggy but the center is still crunchy.
(Antonia Allegra, editor-in-chief, *Napa Valley Appellation*)

Syrah or Zinfandel with old-fashioned spaghetti and meatballs.

Smoked turkey sandwich on wheat bread with mango chutney and Gewurztraminer.

15

The Fine Art of Visiting a Winery

A day touring a wine-making region can be worth weeks of browsing at the wine merchant. In what other situation can you taste and compare many wines at once, at little or no cost, and usually with a knowledgeable person just across the counter from you? You can explore regional similarities and differences, specialties and oddities, strengths and weaknesses.

Wineries run the gamut from one-person operations in warehouses by the railroad tracks to multi-million-dollar chateaux complete with gift shops, restaurants, and vast parking lots. No matter a winery's size, a few simple guidelines will help you get the most out of a visit.

• **First things first: Designate a driver who will not consume alcohol!**

• Don't wear perfume, aftershave or anything else with a strong scent. It will interfere with your own sense of smell and spoil the tasting for anyone near you.

• Use the eyes-nose-mouth system for tasting (*look* at the wine, *smell* the wine, *taste* the wine). Then, if you feel comfortable doing it, spit rather than swallowing. (Most wineries have a "dump bucket" for waste on the counters, and it's perfectly polite to spit into that.) Remember that you're visiting wineries to learn about wine, so you want to be able to taste as much as possible.

At the very least, don't feel obliged to finish every drop of wine in your glass; it's not unusual for some wineries to pour seven or eight samples. Remember that the greatest taste impression comes from sniffing, not swallowing.

• Take time to eat during the day, so you're not drinking on an empty stomach.

• If the staff in a tasting room is not helpful, go elsewhere. Sometimes tasting room workers are terrific, sometimes not. They should be ready and willing to describe wines and answer your questions.

• Try to visit during the off-season (winter or spring) or at least on weekdays. On Fourth of July weekend, you'll just be part of the crowd, lucky to get near the bar for a taste of anything. During a quiet week, though, you'll probably get thoughtful answers to your questions.

• Don't balk at paying to taste wine. Some wineries, especially in busy areas like California's Napa Valley, charge a small fee, but a dollar or two is not much to pay for a great learning experience.

• Keep your goals realistic, and don't try to cover too much ground too quickly. Better to visit two or three wineries and really pay attention than to rush from one to the next and try to figure out later where you've been.

• Don't avoid large wineries. Many of them have excellent tours that explain the details of the winemaking process, something few small wineries are equipped to do.

• Take notes on the wines you like, so you can remember them and look for them after you return home. Some wineries will give you copies of labels, a brochure to take notes on, or even order forms.

• If you fall in love with a wine you taste, buy some. Many wineries pour tastes of wines that you're unlikely to find at your corner wine shop, or special reserve wines made in limited quantities that may only be sold at the winery.

• Don't expect bargains. Generally, tasting room prices are about the same as wine shop retail prices. Discounters back home may sell a wine for a couple of bucks less, but that's not as much fun as buying it at the winery.

• If you find something really special, buy several bottles or even a case. It may seem like a lot at the time, but it's nice to have enough to serve at a dinner party or two. I've often been sorry that I didn't splurge on a couple of extra bottles of a wine I really enjoyed. Most wineries give discounts if you buy a case, and sometimes on a half-case.

• Avoid putting wine in the car if you're touring on a hot summer day. Temperatures can soar past 100 degrees Fahrenheit in a closed trunk or car. By the time you get home, the wine could be cooked beyond all recognition. Bringing along an insulated picnic cooler can help solve the problem.

• If you're buying a lot of wine, find out if the winery will ship to your home. Shipping usually adds about $1 to $2 a bottle, but you won't have to schlep the bottles (wine is heavy), or risk leaving them in the car.

• If shipping's not an option, ask your home wine shop to order a wine you like.

• Don't feel obligated to buy wine from every winery you visit. Winemakers understand that many visitors are fans who have been buying their wines for years. Don't let anyone pressure you into buying wine.

• Sign up for the winery's mailing list, if they have one. Winery newsletters are a great source of information and education, and you can order special releases from wineries you like.

• Once you've had some experience visiting wineries, pick out a favorite and call ahead to make an appointment to see how the wine is made. If you don't call in the middle of harvest season (September and October), many winemakers will be happy to show you around.

Learning with Others:
The Wine-Tasting Group

O ne way to become more confident about wine is to join — or start — a wine-tasting group or wine appreciation class. Just as in a class on any other subject, you'll soon find out that some people know more than you do and some people know less, and that the questions you have are shared by many others.

In most big cities, wine-tasting groups are easy to find. In Seattle, for example, the Pacific Northwest Enological Society has 2,000 members, monthly meetings and a couple of large-scale parties every year. By joining a group, you'll be able to taste dozens of wines, usually for a reasonable fee, and talk them over with fellow tasters. Check the course listings of local colleges and universities for wine appreciation classes, or inquire at your local wine shop.

Getting Organized

A lot of people just get together with six or eight interested friends or colleagues to form their own group, meeting once a month or so on a regular schedule. Everyone agrees on a certain amount of money to pitch in — usually around $10 to 15 a person, depending on the number of participants and how extravagant they want to be in choosing wines. The group could suggest types of wine they want to know more about for a tasting, or the host could come up with an idea. Then that month's host goes to a good wine merchant and chooses four to six bottles that would make for an interesting tasting.

When starting out, you'll want the wines to be markedly different from each other. For instance, you could get six different white varietals: a Chardonnay, a Pinot Gris, a Riesling, a Gewurztraminer, a Sauvignon Blanc and a Chenin Blanc. Or choose several different varietals from the same region, like Cabernet Sauvignon, Merlot, Gamay and Zinfandel from the Napa Valley.

How about the same varietal from several different regions, like Pinot Noir from Burgundy, the Santa Barbara area, Oregon and Australia? Or build the tasting around a food: ask the wine merchant to recommend several distinctive wines that would all go with shellfish, or salmon, or charcoal-grilled steaks. (Of course, this works best when tidbits of the food in question are part of the tasting.) The possibilities are just about endless — and don't forget sherries, ports and dessert wines. As you get more experienced, you can get into more and more subtle distinctions, tasting six barrel-fermented Washington State Chardonnays, for example, or a group of French Champagnes.

The Right Equipment

Since most tastings call for four or five glasses per person, it's easiest to have each group member bring his or her own. Be sure to have pitchers of water available, and a couple of *dump buckets* — large containers, often plastic — for people to empty wine glasses into, and spit into if they're so inclined.

It'll help to hold the tasting in a room with good light, so you can better appreciate the wines' colors, though going all the way with the traditional white tablecloth may be a bit much for casual wine-tasting among friends. Some people like to munch small pieces of French bread or crackers, or cubes of mild cheese, like Swiss, to clear the palate between wines, but a mouthful of

"Fill ev'ry glass, for wine inspires us, and fires us with courage, love and joy."

John Gay,
The Beggar's Opera

water will also do the trick. It's the host's job to make sure the wines are at the right temperature, and to remember the corkscrew.

The Great Cover-Up

During *blind tastings,* the identity of the wines is hidden. This is a usual method of tasting for contests, when it's only fair to hide labels and judge the wines solely on their quality.

Sometimes wine experts have blind tastings just for their own amusement, to see if they can distinguish between different vintages or different wineries. A few people, with lots of experience and great memories, really can pinpoint different wines, sometimes down to the year and the vineyard. But we're all human. One wine writer told the story on himself of trying a *real* blind tasting — he was blindfolded — and being served one red wine and one white wine. He couldn't even tell which was which!

Blind tastings are pretty much pointless for people who are beginning to learn about wine. It's a lot more productive to have the labels visible, so every time you pick up the bottle you're able to read the winery name, varietal and other information. (If you decide you want to try a blind tasting, the classic method is to wrap the bottles in skinny brown paper bags secured at the neck. Using aluminum foil is simpler, but the shape of the bottle may give away clues about which wine is inside).

One group I've heard about turns wine tasting into a contest by holding blind tastings. They agree on a type of wine before the meeting, and then each couple goes out and buys a bottle on their own. They arrive with the bottle wrapped in foil, and each bottle gets a number. After all the sniffing and slurping is over, everybody puts a dollar in a kitty. Group members vote on their favorite wine, the bottle is unveiled, and the couple that brought the favorite wine wins the pot. All the bottles are then unwrapped, so everyone can see which wines they were tasting. Trying to decide which wine is "best" can lead to some interesting

> *A reminder: white wines generally taste fine just out of the refrigerator or slightly warmer; the sweeter the wine, the cooler the recommended serving temperature. Light, young reds tend to taste best between 55 to 60 degrees; full-bodied reds are often drunk at 60 to 65 degrees. You could start with the wines a bit cold, because they'll warm up as group members help themselves.*

discussions, because individual tastes vary so much.

Once you get the group started, try to figure out how to work food into it, perhaps picking out a couple of simple appetizers (such as smoked salmon or Roquefort cheese or grilled chicken skewers with spicy Thai peanut sauce) and paying attention to how they go with the wines. Talk about your perceptions, and listen to fellow group members' opinions.

And remember: if the only time you're drinking wine is at wine tastings, you're missing the point. A wine-tasting group isn't an end in itself. Instead, it's a way to learn about wines and find wines you like. Use the wine-tasting group as a springboard to more wine experiences.

The technical term for a group of wines poured at the same time at a tasting or dinner is a flight. At some wine-society dinners, more than one flight is served. For example, you might taste a flight of several white wines with a first course, a flight of reds with the main course and a third flight of sparkling wines with dessert. I don't know if there's a technical term for a person who survives one of these meals.

17

Putting It All Together

W hich wines are good, and which are not? Almost all books and
magazines about wine are devoted, directly or indirectly, to answering
this question. Wine critics give ratings, winemakers enter contests, judges
bestow medals and merchants hang hefty price tags on bottles that
someone, somewhere, considers better than the competition.

Like everyone, I prefer some wines to others. But I have purposefully
avoided making judgments about quality in this book. It's not that I think
questions of quality are entirely subjective. Judging wine is a lot like judging
Olympic figure-skating. Some of the skaters fall on their butts. Some are so
marvelous that their genius is obvious to anyone. But many more are in-
between — very accomplished, but only the most perceptive judge can
discern the subtle differences in technique and style that result in a gold
medal, a bronze, or no medal at all.

Similarly, some wines fall on their butts, metaphorically speaking,
and it takes only a little experience to recognize their defects. Some are so
magical that agreement on their merits is virtually unanimous. However, in
that huge universe of wines in between, there's plenty of room for
disagreement. Like those graceful skaters, many wines have their ways of
pleasing or impressing.

The only opinion that really matters is your own. When you tune out

Chapter 17

"Be a lamp unto yourself."

Sakyamuni Buddha

all the static of ratings, contests, prices and white-tablecloth restaurants, one basic question remains: does this wine taste good now, in this place, at this time? I hope that after reading this book you feel confident enough to answer that question, and to make judgments based on what's in the bottle, not on what someone else wrote or said about it.

Finally, allow me a comment on that dreaded species, the wine snob. The realm of snootiness is where you find people who know a little, not a lot. I've met people who tell me they'll only drink French wine (or Italian or Australian or German wine) because only the French (insert favorite nationality here) make anything worth drinking. Those guys remind me of some of the European students I used to teach in beginning English classes. They'd insist that the only proper way to speak the language was with a British accent. Then they'd ask me — me, with my hang-ten California accent — if I came from London or Oxford!

Talk to almost any winemaker the world over, and you'll find a person who's as down-to-earth as they come. Most winemakers are at least ninety percent farmer, because making good wine depends on growing good grapes. They stomp around muddy vineyards in grimy jeans and rubber boots, and rarely manage to scrub all the dirt out from under their fingernails. And at the end of the day, when they finally find a moment to pour themselves a glass, sit on the porch and watch the sun set over the vineyard, they aren't thinking about price, ratings and impressing their friends. They simply revel in the pure, joyous taste of the wine.

May you do the same. Cheers!

"Good wine is a necessity of life for me."

Thomas Jefferson

Appendix:
Resources for Learning More

• **At wine appreciation classes and wine-tasting groups**, you can taste many wines for a fraction of the cost of buying a bottle of each. Many community colleges and university extension programs offer classes. The Tasters Guild (1451 W. Cypress Creek Rd., Suite #300-26, Ft. Lauderdale FL 33309, 305-776-4870) is a national organization that publishes *Wine and Spirits* magazine and has local chapters that sponsor tastings and other events. Check with local cooking schools and wine merchants. You also can contact the Society of Wine Educators (132 Shaker Rd., East Longmeadow, MA 01028, 413-567-8272) for information on classes and teachers in your area.

• **Many wine merchants publish free monthly or quarterly newsletters** about good values, new wine releases and tastings or special events at the shop. The newsletter from Kermit Lynch Wine Merchant (1065 San Pablo Ave., Berkeley, CA 94702-1317), a retail shop and nationwide distributor specializing in excellent and often inexpensive wines from small European producers, is a real delight.

• **Many wineries publish occasional free newsletters** announcing new releases and chatting about everyday life in the vineyards. Some are hilarious, some scholarly, some amateurish, and most give you lots of good, inside gossip to amuse your friends with when you serve the wines. Sign the mailing list when you visit a winery, or write to favorite wineries and ask to be added to their lists.

• **Look for wine columns** in national publications like *Bon Appétit* and *Food & Wine*. Your local newspaper may also have a wine columnist. Frank Prial's columns on Wednesdays in the *New York Times* are clear, good-humored and useful for beginners as well as experts.

• **Read magazines devoted to wine,** such as the *Wine Spectator, Wine and Spirits* and *Decanter.*

• **Winemaker dinners** are special meals at restaurants featuring the wines of one winery. As the name implies, the winemaker, up close and personal, is usually the featured attraction, table-hopping and making a short speech (or sometimes an amazingly long one) about the wines being served. Such dinners should give you some good ideas about food and wine combinations, and you'll often taste wines that are older or in limited supply. Depending on the restaurant and the wines, they can cost anywhere from $35 on up, usually in the $60 to $75 per person range. They're often listed in the food pages of local newspapers.

• **The Wine Aroma Wheel** is a laminated circle devised by Ann C. Noble, an expert in sensory evaluation and a professor at the University of California, Davis, which is famed for its *oenology* (wine studies) department. Noble has divided the aromas in wine into 12 categories, like *spicy, chemical* and *fruity,* then subdivided them into more than 50 aromas ranging from the appetizing (like *apricot* and *green olive*) to the repellent (like *dusty* and *sauerkraut*). Consulting the wheel really expands your descriptive vocabulary, and it's fun, too. Available from wine merchants or by mail from Howe Noble Lee Designed, P.O. Box 1817, Healdsburg CA 95448, 707-431-0947.

Among the wealth of books on every aspect of wine, some of my favorites are:

• *Mastering Wine,* Tom Maresca (Grove Press). The only book I've seen that really zooms in on how wine tastes. Maresca's writing is smart and funny as he guides the reader through tasting and comparing more than forty pairs of wines. A real education.

• *Windows on the World Complete Wine Course,* Kevin Zraly (Sterling). Zraly, the former wine buyer at Windows on the World restaurant in New York, is a major figure in wine education nationwide. A useful text covering the wines of many countries quickly and readably.

• *The Vintner's Art,* Hugh Johnson and James Halliday (Simon & Schuster). Johnson is England's grand old man of wine writing. An exhaustive and beautifully illustrated volume that explains in detail how wine is made. Actually, just about anything by Johnson is worth reading.

• *The Commonsense Book of Wine,* Leon D. Adams (Wine Appreciation Guild). An updated favorite by this country's wine writer emeritus. Insightful and interesting, combining a friendly tone with an insider's knowledge.

• *Red Wine with Fish: The New Art of Matching Wine with Food,* David Rosengarten and Joshua Wesson (Simon & Schuster). A bright, amusing treatise on escaping the tyranny of "The Rules" about food and wine. Clear advice on how to enjoy wine the way it should be enjoyed — with food.

• *Adventures on the Wine Route,* Kermit Lynch (Farrar Straus Giroux). An engrossing memoir of Lynch's experiences seeking out wines from small French wineries. A great read, and a great introduction to the romance of wine.

• *Village in the Vineyards,* Thomas Matthews (Farrar Straus Giroux). Matthews, a bureau chief for the *Wine Spectator,* lived for a year in a village in Bordeaux, and wrote a graceful, keenly observed book about life, traditions and winemaking there. With photos by his wife, Sara Matthews.

Index

Index

Index

Index

Riedel glassware, 52

Riesling
    complementary herbs and spices, 62
    description, 25
    pronunciation, 30

Room temperature, 48

Rosengarten, David, 105

Sancerre, 33

Sangiovese, 33

Santa Fe-style foods
    with wines, 59

Sauces
    and wine choices 60

Sauternes
    varietals used, 33

Sauvignon Blanc
    complementary herbs and spices, 62
    description, 25-26
    pronunciation, 30

Savennières, 33

Screwpull, 43

Selecting wine
    for beginners, 39-40

Semillon
    complementary herbs and spices, 62
    description, 25
    pronunciation, 30

Sense(s)
    smell, 4
    taste, 4

Serving
    in restaurants, 85-87
    temperature, 47-48
    sparkling wine, 65-66

Shipping, 95

"Shoulders"
    on bottles, 36

Simpsons,The, 69

Sitwell, Edith, 2

Smelling. 18-19

Snobs, 102

Society of Wine Educators, 103

Sokol Blosser, Susan, 84-85

Sommelier, 81

Sparkling wine, 63-67
    with food, 66
    opening, 68

Sparkling wine, (cont.)
    serving and storing, 65-66

Spoilage, 76-77
    how to recognize, 53-54
    in sparkling wine, 66

Spumante, 65

St.-Joseph, 33

St.-Julien, 33

Steiman, Harvey, 78

Stein, Gertrude, 41

Storage
    leftover wine, 50
    long term, 74
    sparkling wine, 66

Sugar
    residual, 12
    role in pairing food and wine, 57

Supermarket
    wine assistance in, 76

Sweetness, 8, 10-12
    vs. fruitiness, 11-12

Swirling, 19, 49
    technique, 21

Syrah
    complementary herbs and spices, 62
    description, 27
    pronunciation, 30

Tannin, 8-10
    astringency, 10
    role in aging, 71
    role in pairing food and wine, 59
    sensation in mouth, 9
    source in wine, 9

Taste, tasting
    blind, 99
    comparing varietals, 38
    essential elements, 8
    eyes-nose-mouth method, 17-20
    in groups, 97-100
    physiology of, 4
    in restaurants, 38, 86-87
    visiting wineries, 93-94
    in the wine shops, 39

Taste buds, 4

Tasters Guild, 103

Tea tasting, 8-14

Temperature
    effect on aroma, 19
    rate of warming, 48

Index

About the Author

Heidi Yorkshire writes about food, wine and travel for *Bon Appétit* and many other national publications. She also teaches Wine Savvy Seminars on tasting, buying and enjoying wine. A member of the Society of Wine Educators, she conducts classes for groups ranging from gatherings of wine and food professionals to beginners interested in learning more about wine.

Wine Savvy was one of three nominees for the best wine, beer or spirits book in the Julia Child Cookbook Awards. The book has been published in Japanese by YoYoSha. Yorkshire is co-author of the award-winning cookbook, *Desserts by Nancy Silverton* (HarperCollins), and *Cooking with Olive Oil in the New World* (Bantam, 1997)

A native of Los Angeles, Yorkshire lived for several years in Paris, and is now at home in Portland, Oregon, with her husband, writer Joseph Anthony, and her cat, Bruiser. You can reach her through Duplex Media Group (P.O. Box 12081, Portland, OR 97212) or by e-mail at winesavvy@aol.com.

Order Form

Please send _____ copy/copies of *Wine Savvy: The Simple Guide to Buying and Enjoying Wine, Anytime, Anywhere* at $12.95 each.

Name_____

Address _____

City _____State _____Zip _____

Phone_____

Shipping

Book Rate: $2.50 for the first book, and $1.00 for each additional book. (Delivery by book rate shipping may take up to four weeks.)

Priority Mail: $4.00 for up to 4 books to same address.

Book total: $ _____

Shipping: $ _____

Total amount: $ _____

For mail orders, make checks payable to:

Duplex Media Group
and mail to P.O. Box 12081, Portland OR 97212-0081.

For VISA, Mastercard or Discover orders, mail, fax to 503/280-8964 or e-mail to winesavvy@aol.com

Card # _____ Signature: _____

Exp: _____ / _____ Name on card: _____